THE
STORY
CURE

THE
STORY
CURE

A Book Doctor's Pain-Free Guide to Finishing Your Novel or Memoir

DINTY W. MOORE

TEN SPEED PRESS
California | New York

*To the many writers who have asked
for my help, considered my advice,
and, in the end, taught me so much.*

CONTENTS

Introduction

It has been my good fortune these past thirty years to not only be a writer, but to also teach writing, to students of all ages and all backgrounds, in a variety of settings. Some students come to me eager to complete their first short story or essay, while others arrive having already started on a first book.

People often say that "everybody has a book in them." I can't tell you whether that is true or not—I haven't met *everybody*. But I can tell you that the folks I'm privileged to work with do have a book in them, and most are willing to work hard to get that book out into the world.

My job is to help them. And I very much enjoy doing it.

Before exploring the Story Cure and how it can lead a writer from start to finish in creating a successful book, let me say a few words about what is meant by the term Book Doctor.

A common enough term in the writing world, Book Doctor is used to describe a person who will take a book manuscript— perhaps an early draft of a novel or memoir, perhaps draft sixteen—and diagnose why it is not yet working.

"Not yet working" might mean the author herself is dissatisfied, sensing that the overall arc of the book isn't falling gracefully into place or the main character is not coming to life on the page. Alternatively, "not yet working" might mean the author has sent a finished draft out to dozens of literary agents or editors, a draft she thought was healthy and ready to go, but has received only polite but impersonal "No thank you" notes, and is now discouraged and wondering "What do they see wrong with my book that I don't see?"

A Book Doctor is different from a copyeditor or proofreader. The task at hand is not to clean up sentences, adjust punctuation, or fix typographical errors. A Book Doctor looks at the patient as a whole—the plot, the main characters, the voice, the structure—or, to continue the physician metaphor, the arms, the legs, the belly, and the heart. The Doctor's job is to diagnose exactly why the patient isn't thriving.

If you've been to a doctor, you can guess what comes next: doctors are full of advice, and they invariably send you out the door with a prescription or two. Sometimes the treatment is simple and quick; other times it can be radical: a transfusion, a transplant, or even an amputation.

A Book Doctor can also sometimes act the part of psychiatrist, helping authors tackle various self-inflicted problems.

Though writing should be a stimulating, rewarding endeavor, for too many it can lead to self-doubt and, worse yet, self-loathing. Writing well is difficult enough—drafting twenty or two hundred pages takes devotion, attention, and a healthy dose of stubbornness—but it becomes excruciatingly tough when we let rampaging anxiety poison the experience.

This Book Doctor, however, believes that whatever is ailing a novel or memoir in progress is *not* about the writer, it is about the story: how well we understand it, how well we tell it, and how well we enable it to come alive in the reader's mind. That's the heart of the Story Cure.

And what is meant by the word "pain-free" in this book's subtitle?

Well, writing is painstaking, meaning the writer must take great care and pay close attention to every detail, every word. But it should *not* be painful. And if it is painful, it probably hurts most because the author is letting the negative voices of doubt overrun the exhilaration of creativity and discovery.

We'll address that as well.

This book is designed for writers at the beginning of their novel or memoir project, those somewhere in the middle, as well as those who have completed multiple drafts. The goal is to get you to the finish line, to make sure you complete your book and have something in your hands that you can feel proud of.

Even if you are well along in your project, through a first or second draft, I recommend beginning at the beginning of this guide. Understanding how the "heart story" can strengthen all aspects of your novel or memoir will be helpful throughout each stage of drafting and revision.

But no one ever reached the finish while sitting at the starting line trying on sneakers.

So let's get started.

Part I

CURES

["We tell ourselves stories in order to live."

–JOAN DIDION[1]]

1 | THE STORY CURE

DIAGNOSING PROBLEMS OF THE HEART

A key piece of the Story Cure is the understanding that what you *should* be focusing on in your novel or memoir is storytelling, pure and simple. The most direct way to make your book one that readers want to read (and, in that way, one that editors want to publish) is to tell a damn good story.

Too often, we lose track of that.

Too often I meet writers halfway into a book project who no longer feel confident in the story they want to tell, or more importantly, no longer feel entirely sure why someone should want to hear it.

I know from experience that it is all too easy to lose track. Perhaps losing track is an integral part of the process. But knowing what track you are on, and getting back onto that track when the process veers off, is a critical skill for any writer.

What Is Story?

Remember this: stories that keep readers fully engaged and eager to follow along through each moment and every surprising turn did not begin with Charles Dickens, Stephen King, or J. K. Rowling. Captivating storytelling goes back to the origins of language itself, to humankind's earliest days.

Long before printing presses and book clubs, our ancestors kept fear at bay by telling stories—of heroic hunts, of memorable victories, and of mysterious, powerful gods. While the hunting and fighting stories were likely based on either memory or ancestral lore, the tales of gods and goddesses mark the beginnings of imaginative fiction. How to explain thunder, floods, birth, death, the inexplicable movement of the sun? Our ancestors created stories to explain these. Stories that gave them both understanding and solace.

Author Barry Lopez says that stories are part mystery, part ministry, and absolutely indispensable. "We need them, I believe, in the way we need water, if we are to revive ourselves in this harrowing time" he writes. "The reason we tell stories . . . is to keep each other from being afraid."[2]

Novelist Ben Percy believes that the most enduring stories reach readers at the deepest level by taking "a knife to the nerve of the moment."[3] Mary Wollstonecraft Shelley's *Frankenstein*—the story of a mad doctor who uses electricity to create a superhuman monster—found its root power by reflecting people's fears of the industrial revolution, while Jack Finney's *The Body Snatchers*—later made into the movie *Invasion of the Body Snatchers*—connected directly to mid-twentieth-century fears of communist spies infiltrating small-town America.

Percy's own book *Red Moon* begins with a man on a commercial jetliner inexplicably transforming into a werewolf and attacking his fellow passengers. This transformation is happening not just on the one plane, but simultaneously on two other airplanes, one of which crashes into a wheat field.

Does that sound at all familiar?

"We fear, more than anything, terrorism and disease," Percy explains, "and I braided the two together."[4]

Not all stories are horror stories, of course, and not all books focus so directly on humankind's greatest fears. The enduring ones, however, still find their power by addressing intrinsic human concerns, those vexing problems that keep us awake and thinking late into the night.

Jane Austen's *Pride and Prejudice* features neither werewolves nor body snatchers. Instead, this tale of five unmarried daughters in nineteenth-century England and the eligible bachelors who come calling enchanted—*and still enchants*—readers by reflecting upon enduring concerns about class, gender, and morality. The *Harry Potter* series is about more than schoolchildren and magic spells; it explores the power of self-sacrifice and the importance of tolerance. Alice Walker's *The Color Purple* is, on the surface, the story of African-American women living a generation or two beyond slavery, but the underlying issues of prejudice and family violence resonate with readers of any race, any age, any time.

That is why people tell stories, and why we listen to the good ones with such rapt attention. Stories revive us, challenge us, startle us, and offer us new ways to reflect upon our world and the moment's most perplexing questions.

All of this, by the way, is every bit as true of the memoir as it is of the novel.

Think, for instance, of Cheryl Strayed's *Wild: From Lost to Found on the Pacific Crest Trail* (a book that spent 126 weeks on the *New York Times* best-seller list). *Wild* tells the story of Strayed's solo—and fairly reckless—1,100-mile hike from the Mojave Desert to the Oregon-Washington border, and of the personal tragedies that led her to take the risk: a failed marriage and a mother who had recently died of rapid-spreading lung cancer.

That's quite a story in and of itself, but there are deeper themes, more powerful currents, at play.

Joseph Campbell's classic study of comparative mythology, *The Hero with a Thousand Faces*, traces myths so powerful that they have survived for thousands of years and finds that such stories follow a common trajectory: a hero starts in the "ordinary world," receives "a call to adventure," leading to a "special world" where he—in the old days, it was always a "he"—faces tasks and trials, leading eventually to one great challenge. The surviving hero ultimately leaves the "special world" to return to the ordinary, a changed person with new resolve, understanding, or power.

Strayed's book follows this pattern closely—a woman facing trials and sorrows goes on a heroine's journey, enters the special world of the Pacific Crest Trail, and fights to survive the long walk for which she was untrained and unprepared.

Strayed herself readily acknowledges this connection to mythical story, reminding other writers, and her students, to "remember the ancients."

"Nobody *should* read my book," she says, "because I took an interesting hike and I loved my mom a lot and she died. That's just a very small, insignificant story—insignificant to anyone but me. And so my job, as a writer, was to make it about other people."[5]

Strayed allowed the story of one woman's ambitious backpacking adventure to become "about other people" by focusing on the primal elements of her story, those emotions and ambitions shared across humankind.

Readers who have not lost a mother to lung cancer, who are not reeling from a failed marriage, still feel Strayed's story as their own because we've all experienced loss, experienced sorrow, and felt the need for a transformative experience.

What Is *Your* Heart Story?

A quick but important clarification: story is different from plot or structure. *The Story Cure* will address plot and structure, how they interact and the rich opportunities they present, in chapter 6, but what we are discussing here is the *primal* story, the fundamental human tale that is being told, the problem of the heart.

So, let's say that your novel-in-progress has a main character, a few secondary characters, and a setting. In your early drafts, you set out to describe the characters and the place, and the characters interact, move around in the world. (If, instead, your main character spends two hundred pages sitting alone in an isolation booth brooding on deep philosophical conundrums, you may have a problem.)

Perhaps this novel is set in one of your favorite spots—the Outer Banks of North Carolina, a farm much like your great-grandparents' farm in Iowa, or the ethnic Chicago neighborhood where you spent your earliest years. The main character, maybe, is a child roughly modeled on the child that you once were, or a woman like your grandmother, or just a character you've devised who combines traits from many people.

Where's your story?

One of my favorite writers, Kurt Vonnegut, once advised, "Every character should want something, even if it is only a glass of water."[6]

That is, in fact, the best place to start.

What does your main character want?

On page one, it may *just be* a glass of water. Or maybe a gin and tonic, if it's been a bad day.

But the thirst has to go deeper quickly, and the glass of water must come to represent a basic human aspiration, fear, or desire within the first few pages.

If you can't define what it is your character wants, then you likely have no story.

Maybe your character wants a lot of things—new shoes, a clean suit, a ride into Cedar Rapids, a job interview, a paycheck. That's fine, but what do those desires represent? What journey is he about to take, and what obstacles are going to slow him down? I can imagine a number of currents that might flow underneath the story of the young man who wants new shoes and a ride into Cedar Rapids. It might be the need to battle self-doubt brought on by childhood trauma, a reaction to his father's harsh and constant criticism, a secret dream to live a life far different than the one for which he seems destined on the family farm. Something universal. Something others have felt as well.

Knowing this last element—where the character's story and struggles will connect directly with other readers, other human beings—is what will allow you to write a book where every scene, every line of dialogue, each turn in each and every chapter, makes sense, moves the story forward, and gives the reader an emotional connection to your words and descriptions. It is what makes readers turn the page.

The opposite of what I am trying to illustrate here is a novel where "stuff just happens." The narrator goes to the park and has a conversation, then he goes home and makes a pot of chili, and then he heads over to the neighborhood tavern, chats with a guy named Louie, and watches a ballgame, and then he goes home to sleep. In the morning he makes eggs and toast and then drives to the pier and stares into the ocean. Later he sits in a coffee shop and watches people walk by.

I've seen books that ramble along in such a fashion, rough drafts that "just aren't working" in this way. The author describes people in pleasing detail, uses graceful language, conjures the reflection of light off the still ocean surface quite poetically, but why? What's going on?

My diagnosis: The author doesn't know the deeper story, or has misplaced it somehow.

You might think memoirists don't have this problem. They aren't making up moments in the main character's life, inventing passersby at the coffee shop, devising watershed events, because they are writing about what has actually occurred. What I've observed over the years, however, is that memoirists often have an even tougher time with story than do novelists.

Why?

In my experience, it is because some voice in the memoirist's head keeps insisting, *These things really happened, so my job is simple: just write it down as accurately as I can, in the right order, and it will be fascinating.*

But that's not enough.

I regularly meet students, in weekend workshops or individual coaching sessions, who explain that they have begun writing a memoir about their mother, or grandmother, because "she led a very fascinating life." Or they tell me that they are going to write a book about their own lives, "because so many unbelievable things have happened."

I suspect that the author, her mother, or her Granny Jane did have a fascinating life, full of remarkable events, because most of us do, whether we realize it or not. For the memoir to be successful, however, the writer has to know what human current runs deep under the story he or she is about to tell.

By way of illustration, here's a memoir that likely won't be attracting boatloads of readers anytime soon:

> My mother was born in Chicago in 1928, and then this happened to her, and then this happened to her, and then this other thing happened to her, and then she got married, and then my parents moved to Philadelphia, and then this happened, and then this happened, and then I was born. My father got a promotion at work and wasn't around much. And then this happened, and then this, and so on.

This is not a story. It is a mere listing of events. Now here is a memoir that very well may fill quite a few boats:

> My mother struggled all of her life with a deep shame because of her family's poverty, and this shame led her to make numerous decisions she would come to regret, until one day I was astonished to witness [think Hero's Journey here] my mother's courage as she found her way through the sorrow and crippling embarrassment to reach redemption, refusing to let her deep shame drive her life's choices anymore.

(Or maybe the mother never did come through, and the true Hero's Journey is how the author, the woman's daughter, though deeply connected to her mother's pain and sadness, was able herself to move on, refusing to fall into the same unhealthy cycle of embarrassment and self-doubt.)

You can remove the word "poverty" in this example and substitute addiction problems, spousal abuse, ethnic or racial prejudice, physical imperfection, or any one of the countless reasons we are led to feel less worthy than other people. But whatever the situation, knowing that the primal story, the heart of it all, is the struggle to overcome shame brought on by events outside of the woman's control—we can't choose our families, or easily dismantle societal prejudice—allows the author of the memoir to carefully choose which events in her life and her mother's life need to be on the page.

At the same time, knowing the heart of the story helps the author see which events—though they may have been quite interesting, or are remembered well, or have been retold many times in the family—don't actually belong in *this* book, because they don't move the story forward in any powerful way.

A memoir is not *everything* that happened in your life; rather, it is those moments that tell the story best.

Discovering (or Rediscovering) the Heart of Your Story

I've admittedly been quite generous with my metaphors here—the heart story, the Book Doctor, the Hero's Journey—but please allow me one more:

The Invisible Magnetic River.

For all of the years that I've been teaching storytelling in college classrooms and summer workshops, the writers in the room more often than not find it easy to grasp terms like character, setting, plot, and dialogue, but all of us—myself included—struggle when it comes to terms like "meaning" and "theme."

What does a story *mean*?

To be honest, I hate that question. Too many of us were taught in high school or college to approach a work of literature as if it were a puzzle. As if once we figure out what it means, we can close the book.

But that's not why we read. Reading great stories is an experience, not a mere gathering of information.

To my mind, the use of the term "theme" is even worse. It suggests a moral lesson, inserted by the author (usually a dead white male author), something about man, or nature, or perhaps an immense symbolic bleached creature of the sea. It suggests that instead of writing compelling stories, we are all just writing sermons, cautionary lessons to instruct the unwashed masses.

So eventually I devised my own metaphor to replace "meaning" or "theme," my own way of trying to guide writers toward the intuitive cloudbank of emotion, metaphor, image, and idea that makes a piece of fiction or nonfiction, novel or memoir, more than just a collection of scenes or observations, but something greater than the sum of its many parts.

How does a piece of writing open up into something wide and powerful, or reflect a deeper truth that is, to quote the poet Langston Hughes, "older than the flow of human blood in human veins"?[7]

That's where the Invisible Magnetic River comes in.

Every good story, to my mind, has one.

Why Invisible?

Because thesis sentences are dull, flat, and awkward.

Because once you say a thing out loud it often becomes less potent.

Because a truth you discover for yourself will always be more powerful than a truth someone else tries to impose upon you.

Because in a story, or memoir, or novel, the truth is sometimes not in the words, but between them, in the sheer, permeable tissue that runs from moment to moment.

Because sometimes, more often than you think, an author may begin her project not fully aware of the truths her book will eventually reveal, those deeper currents that flow up from the subconscious, surprising, at times, the writer herself.

Why Magnetic?

Because everything—words, images, scenes, snippets of dialogue, reflection—everything on the page should be drawn toward the Invisible River. Not snapped into place. Not riveted to a beam, or forced into a straight line, but pulled down, gently encouraged to lean in toward the river's flow.

Because if the moment on the page does not lean in toward the Invisible River of emotional resonance, the moment does not belong in the book.

Because if there is no magnetic pull, then all you have is words.

Why a River?

Rivers start small, but gain strength with every mile, flowing tenaciously forward toward an end that can't be seen before arriving.

Rivers insist on finding their own way toward that unseen end, carving through whatever soft sand, hard clay, or rigid shale is found lining the banks.

Rivers don't follow a straight line. Rivers meander, change speed, widen in spots and grow narrower in others, deepen here and turn shallower there.

Rivers do all of this, but in the end they are always moving downstream, always taking up whatever is found along the way and carrying it along.

And though the occupants of a boat on that river may not know where they are headed, the current always knows.

Locating the Invisible Magnetic River in your story early on is, to my mind, the best way of making sure your primal story is controlling the narrative flow. Don't panic, however, if you notice the currents of that river beginning to shift along the way. In fact, the current you identify as central in the early draft of your novel or memoir may turn out to be a secondary current, and the main current that you discover along the way may be far more powerful. A real river is fluid, and this one is as well.

The River gives your story crucial momentum, but of equal importance, finding this Invisible River flowing underneath your heart story allows you to navigate the myriad choices facing you both intuitively and wisely. If a particular word, scene, image, or metaphor is not drawn toward the River, not sharing the magnetic pull, then it is probably not the right word, scene, image, or metaphor.

Or as Joseph Conrad once put it, "A work that aspires, however humbly, to the condition of art should carry its justification in every line."[8]

Yes, "every line" is a daunting goal, but it is doable. What is needed is time, effort, and the willingness to forgive yourself when you mess up a bit.

✚ THE BOOK DOCTOR MAKES A HOUSE CALL

The Cure for Common Story Problems

Most likely this has happened to you. You've gone to a doctor's waiting room, learned from the preoccupied woman at the front desk that the doctor is running forty-five minutes late, and dejectedly faced the only two choices available: grab a two-year-old magazine about fishing, even though you don't own a boat (the doctor has two!), or just sit there and stare at posters on the wall illustrating in microscopic detail all of the horrible ailments threatening your frail human body.

Well, good news. This Book Doctor makes house calls, and he almost never asks for blood or urine samples. So relax a bit, while I run through some of the more common story problems facing memoirists and novelists.

❶ DIAGNOSIS: This Book Has No (Heart) Story

Not all stories have to connect emotionally with mankind's deepest darkest concerns, in the manner of *Frankenstein* or Ben Percy's *Red Moon*, but every story needs to connect emotionally with *some* concern common to most of us.

Underneath the words, sentences, scenes, and chapters of your novel or memoir, there needs to be a journey (what Joseph Campbell calls a Hero's Journey). This doesn't mean your primary character has to slay a dragon, but the character does have to face some challenge, universal or personal, and the reader needs to see how your character struggles to overcome that challenge and flourish.

Cheryl Strayed's main character in *Wild*—who, because it is a memoir, is Strayed herself—took her personal struggle with crippling, confusing grief onto the Pacific Crest Trail. But you don't always need that sort of heroic physical journey; exceptional memoirs have been written where the challenge stays much closer to home: a child's struggle with feelings of inadequacy because his family suffers acute poverty, an adult balancing anger with feelings of unworthiness at the end of a marriage or love affair, a partner or parent burdened with guilt because they sometimes resent the complexities of living life alongside someone ill or disabled. Every reader has experienced feelings of self-doubt, guilt, and anger, even if the circumstances differ.

A memoir might also focus less on challenging, adverse experiences and more on our aspirations: moving to Appalachian Ohio and becoming a sheep farmer in order to live a life that feels more authentic, or leaving behind our bulky life possessions and settling down on an island off the coast of Greece to redefine our sense of self. We share common dreams as much as we share common fears.

The novelist has the advantage of being able to artificially create a heroic task for the main character and, if working in the fantasy realm, perhaps eradicating malevolent dragons *is* the best solution. But the killing of that dragon still works best when it represents some deeper emotional truth: slaying gender inequity, or slaughtering deeply held fears and limitations.

But just as all memoirs don't need epic hikes through dangerous terrain, not all novels need swords and giant lizards. Think again of *Pride and Prejudice*, that "quiet book" about unmarried sisters and possible suitors. The "dragon" in Elizabeth Bennett's life wore lace cuffs and a gentleman's waistcoat, or in a wider sense, the novel's fire-breathing antihero was society's strict views on gender roles, propriety, and class. Elizabeth's own journey, of course, was to overcome her own unacknowledged pride and hidden prejudice.

Big or small, frightening or inspiring, you need to identify *some* primal concern or desire in your book, or else the hundreds of pages run the risk of being just a series of events, to no purpose, and readers will quickly lose track of why they are reading.

➤ THE CURE

What does your character want?

Maybe your character wants that dragon dead—the big, smelly green one who keeps shooting flames out of his mouth and scaring the bejeebers out of everyone in the village. Maybe your character wants that dragon dead because her parents, grandparents, nieces, and nephews live in that village, and she hopes someday to raise her own family there. Maybe what your character really wants is safety, and a life not dictated by fear. We all want safety, for ourselves and for our loved ones, and we all battle fears large and small, so your reader—even if she lives in a world where dragons don't roam free—will feel the primal connection.

Maybe your character wants to live outside the strictures of polite nineteenth-century British society, or maybe your character (or you, if this is a memoir) yearns to escape the suffocating atmosphere of an abusive marriage or of an authoritarian religious community.

Maybe your character wants to raise sheep, work with his hands, step away from the computer screen and endless abstract responsibilities and live more closely tied to the rhythms of the natural world. Perhaps this is tied to his childhood, to a memory of his father or grandfather, to some emotional absence in his current life.

A good story—true or fictional—is one that produces in the reader a visceral desire to know what happens next. If the reader doesn't know what your character desires most, deep down, not just practically (a glass of water, a winning lottery ticket) but emotionally, the reader won't have that visceral desire either.

If you are still struggling to define the heart story (or Invisible River) underneath your novel or memoir, find the most important character in the book and determine what he or she really wants to happen (not throughout her entire life, but during the time period covered in the book's two hundred or three hundred pages). Once you know what is most wanted, think about the emotions, needs, disappointments, and psychological complexities that might underpin the desire. It is never as simple as saying, "My character wants a new job" followed by "She got the job and everything is fine." (*Plus, that's just not interesting.*) Why is the change or accomplishment so important, on a deeper, not merely practical, level?

And remember this: if your character doesn't have a strong need or desire, you'll need to invent one, or you'll likely do better telling another story.

❾ DIAGNOSIS: A Wandering, Rambling Story

The book with no heart story is often just a series of events happening to a character who has no clear desire or fear, but sometimes the problem is the precise opposite: your character wants and fears too much. Your character is conflicted on every page. Instead of a heart, he has an erratic, overfiring nervous system, and the central journey is more of a maze than a river.

Charles Dickens's *David Copperfield* clocks in at around 426 pages, depending on which edition you buy; the novel covers the protagonist's life from birth to adulthood, chronicling innumerable adventures, setbacks, unexpected turns, and startling coincidences. Throughout the book, however, running underneath every scene, every chapter (like an underground stream), we understand that Copperfield wants one thing most: an end to the abuse of the weak and helpless (orphans, debtors, the mentally ill) by wealthy and powerful forces.

Copperfield has numerous goals and adventures, but each of these reflects back on his basic wish for fairness. The heart of the character and the heart of the book are connected and clear.

⟹ THE CURE

Can't unravel the many desires and fears of your main character? Does the hero ramble about aimlessly, or does the story start and stop with sharp jolts? Is your protagonist's primary motivation changing from scene to scene, or chapter to chapter?

You need to make a list of the various, perhaps clearly connected or seemingly unrelated, fears and desires of your main character.

(Remember, if you are writing a memoir, *you* are the main character. More on this in chapter 3, but for now, let the word "character" remind you that even though you are real, not imaginary, it is every bit as important in a memoir as it is in a novel to paint a full portrait of yourself, both physical and emotional—just as Dickens did for his hero in *David Copperfield*. Before reading the book, the reader has never met the fictional Copperfield. Well, unless you are writing for a tiny audience of close friends, the reader has never met you, either.)

Once you've made that list, you need to look at the relative strengths of each item, examining which desires or fears are perhaps subcurrents of the primary journey or river. (There is a prompt at the end of this chapter designed to help you do this effectively.)

Eventually, you may need to get out the scalpel and cut away the parts that aren't contributing to the health of the two-hundred-page patient.

THE SILVER LINING

To go along with the listing and prioritizing activity, and to make the excisions less painful, you should remind yourself that this current project need not be the only book you ever write. Tell yourself, in as firm a voice as possible, "All of these things concern me, but in *this* book I need to focus on a particular current, an underlying emotion connected directly to the heart."

(If you are in a crowded coffee shop when you say this to yourself, and the other patrons turn around and look at you oddly, just smile, wink, and stick out your tongue. That way, they'll have a story to tell too, when they meet up with their friends later.)

One advantage to believing that you have more than just one book in you is that you'll have a better, more focused first book. The other is that you've just given yourself a hearty vote of confidence.

Of course there will be another book. You may write three, or thirty.

You are (or will be with hard work and practice) that good.

❷ DIAGNOSIS: Forgetting the Reader

There are many books written every year, and as we all know, not all of them are published, and even some of those that are published don't seem to find more than the tiniest share of readers.

It is all too easy to get caught up in our own stories, and it is not necessarily bad to get carried away in the swell, to become captivated by our own tales. What *is* a problem, however, is staying in that state of enthrallment for the entire drafting, revising, re-revising, and completing-the-book process.

At some point—and I think the exact point where this happens varies from writer to writer—the rose-colored glasses need to come off and what I like to call the "gruff and exacting New York City editor" hat has to be placed firmly atop your head. You need to dispense some tough love, to yourself and to your assembled sentences and pages.

In the end, people aren't going to read your book merely because you spent so much time on it, and they aren't going to read your book because you really, really want them to.

People are going to read your book, and buy copies for their friends, and recommend it to their book club, because you've captivated the reader on every page, in every sentence.

➤ THE CURE

The cure for "forgetting the reader," not surprisingly, is to remember them.

Deliberately.

With pen in hand.

What this means is going over every sentence—yes, *every* sentence—of your manuscript, maybe in the third draft, maybe in the thirteenth, and asking yourself:

- Does the reader need to know this?

- Does the reader already know this?

- Have I told the reader this five times already? (Or written three scenes that convey essentially the same thing?)

- Is the reader confused by this sentence because there is some crucial related detail the reader doesn't yet know, because I've somehow forgotten to tell the reader?

- Is the reader nodding off, because even though I think all of this information is crucial, I've just spent three pages on exposition and nothing much is happening to keep the reader awake?

- Am I telling the reader all of this because it seemed like a good idea in draft four, but now that I look more closely, this scene/chapter/description/conversation doesn't actually connect with my Hero's Journey, primal story, or Invisible Magnetic River (all three of which are essentially names for the same thing—the heartbeat of your book)?

And that's just covering how you provide information to the reader. The next step has to do with the rhythm and music of your prose. That calls for questions like:

- So, yes, this *is* something the reader needs and wants to know, but have I taken three sentences to reveal this to the reader when it could have been relayed far better in one more carefully drafted sentence?

- Am I telling the reader too much? Do I instead need to write some scenes, so the reader can discover for herself and see my character with her own eyes?

- Sure, the story is moving along just fine, but is the language active, are the nouns and verbs lively, the descriptions sensory and vivid?

We'll deal more with the vivacity of your prose style, with nouns and verbs and sensory description, and with all the endless other questions you need to ask in subsequent chapters. But for now, ask yourself the questions just listed, slowly, as you read each sentence of your draft back to yourself.

Yes, this takes time. But it is time very well spent.

And when you are done, revise accordingly. Revise as if someone will lock you away for five years in a world without books or puppies or chocolate or red wine (whatever your biggest weakness is) if your writing is not lighting and delighting every inch of the readers' neural pathways.

PROMPTS AND EXERCISES TO CURE STORY PROBLEMS

While adding new pages to your book or polishing what you already have is usually the best way to make progress, it is sometimes a good idea to step away (or open a new file on your desktop) to do some free-writing or ask yourself some questions. The prompts and exercises that follow are designed to head you in the right direction.

FINDING YOUR BOOK'S JOURNEY

Maybe you weren't really sure of your main character's journey when you began writing. You were so anxious to get your book started, perhaps daydreaming far ahead to the completion, and publication, the late-night call from Oprah, and those gleaming buckets of cash dropped at your doorstep, that you headed off with a vague idea, a sense of what might fill the pages of the book but no sense of how these pages might captivate a wide swath of readers.

I know this happens, because I've done it myself. I call it "Wishful Thinking Disease."

The best way to determine "What does my character want?"—and the flip side—"What does my character definitely *not* want?"—is to make a list.

Don't hold anything back, at least not at the beginning. List everything, big and small (including Vonnegut's glass of water):

My character wants _____.

My character wants _____.

My character wants _____.

My character wants _____.

My character wants _____.

My character definitely does not want _____.

My character definitely does not want _____.

My character definitely does not want _____.

My character definitely does not want _____.

My character definitely does not want _____.

Once you've filled in all of the character's needs, fears, and desires (you will likely need more than the ten fill-in-the-blank statements I've provided here), indicate the two or three strongest desires or fears with dark circles or thick underlining. Remember that the book you are writing covers a specific time period, so the primary question should be what your character wants or does not want during the time period covered by this book, not the character's (or memoirist's) entire life.

Remembering *David Copperfield*—a book crowded with the title character's desires, fears, and needs, yet all of them fitting clearly under one big umbrella—see if you can identify an overarching desire (freedom, love, an end to feelings of shame and unworthiness, fresh adventure and renewal)) that overshadows or encompasses all of the rest.

If you cannot narrow it down to a pivotal, powerful "My character wants _____" statement, one underneath which all the others can be conveniently and clearly nested, you likely need to get to know your main character better. (And yes, this is true even if you are a memoirist, and that main character is you.)

YOU STILL CAN'T FIND IT?

"Over the years I've discovered that all the stories I've told, all the stories I will ever tell, are connected to me in some way," author Isabel Allende has written. "If I'm talking about a woman in Victorian times who leaves the safety of her home and comes to the Gold Rush in California, I'm really talking about feminism, about liberation, about the process I've gone through in my own life, escaping from a Chilean, Catholic, patriarchal, conservative, Victorian family and going out into the world."[9]

What Allende reminds us of here is a simple but crucial truth: in a novel, whether partly autobiographical or entirely imagined, or a memoir, the power of the story you tell is going to flow from you, the writer; those fears and desires you feel most deeply are the fears and desires that will provide your book with force and energy, pulling the reader into every page.

So if you've struck out on the first prompt I offered, if you simply cannot find a powerful "My character wants _____" statement, if the character you've devised just shrugs and mutters, "I honestly don't know what I want here," you likely need to spend some time away from the keyboard, thinking honestly about what *you* fear most and what *you* most care about.

Here's a list of fill-in-the blanks for you:

What I most want is_____.

What I most want is_____.

What I most want is_____.

What I most want is_____.

What I most want is_____.

What I most fear is_____.

What I most fear is_____.

What I most fear is_____.

What I most fear is_____.

What I most fear is_____.

What I am most carefully avoiding is_____.

Keep going until you find what will sustain you over the long process of drafting a book. And then revisit your character (or the "you" on the page in your memoir) and connect character to story.

I KNOW MY STORY BUT NOT HOW TO TELL IT

Story, structure, and plot are inevitably intertwined, and sometimes, quite honestly, they seem a Gordian knot. Unfortunately, there is no simple formula or answer to the question of how you take your character's chief concern—her heroic journey—and structure it from scene to scene, page to page, chapter to chapter. Writing would be so much easier (but perhaps less fascinating and addictive) if such a formula existed.

Even seasoned writers, the lucky few who have published numerous books and have earned a cadre of loyal readers, will tell you that each book is different, that each story has to find its own way. Trial and error is why writing takes so much effort.

Trial and error, though, are also a writer's best friends. Keep trying, keep trusting, and the best answer will eventually present itself. Here's hoping that happens sooner rather than later, but you'll have to expect more than a few false starts.

While searching for the best way to tell your story, write the following advice from author Kenneth Atchity onto an index card, and tape it to the side or your desk:

"Tell your story as though you were trying to keep people awake."[10]

Granted, that's easier said than done. To help yourself reach that goal, take a few minutes (or half an hour) at this point in the writing process and list the moments in your novel or memoir where the scene—what is actually happening between and among the key players in your story—will be most likely to hold the reader's interest. By that, I mean areas that are *not* mere exposition, *not* flatly related backstory, *not* static explanation or interpretation. I mean heated disagreements, unexpected turns of events, fraught conversations, crushing setbacks, surprise arrivals, hiking boots flying off the edge of a cliff.

List these, tape that list to the wall next to Atchity's quote, and from time to time over the coming months check the list to be certain that the book you are writing is centered around these dramatic events. Your book will be all the better for it.

"You start at the stupid end of the book, and if you're lucky you finish at the smart end."

—SALMAN RUSHDIE[1]

2 | YOUR FIRST BREATH

WHERE STORY BEGINS

We can't, no matter how much we sometimes wish that we could, finish our book until we begin it.

That may seem too obvious to mention, but I've encountered more than a few folks in my classes and workshops who have been *talking about* the book they are going to write for years, and who quite sincerely intend to get to that first page "any time now."

The solution to that problem is refreshingly easy: lock yourself behind a closed door this weekend and start.

Harder to solve, however, is the dilemma faced by writers who *have* started, and yet can't seem to make progress because the beginning of their book just doesn't seem right. The opening sentences or pages simply won't cooperate; they refuse to sort themselves out.

This chapter will take a look at opening lines and opening impulses in novels and memoirs, and look as well at strategies to avoid the sort of wheel-spinning that occurs when a writer finds herself bogged down in the first chapter with no clear path forward.

One of my first writing teachers was the novelist Vance Bourjaily, and he found me in exactly that spot.

"I'm trying to nail down my opening chapter," I complained to him one autumn afternoon as he sorted through the day's mail in his bright but cluttered office. "I've tried a hundred different approaches, and none of them seems right."

Vance at the time had already published nearly a dozen books, including one nominated for a National Book Award.

He was a small man, a quick thinker, good-humored, and he seldom wasted words.

"Oh, I never bother with the first chapter," he chuckled matter-of-factly, "until I've finished the whole book. Then I write it."

I was momentarily speechless.

"How do you know where to start," he continued, "until you know where you're headed?"

I was young, perplexed, but eager to look intelligent to my teacher, so I probably said something like, "Well that's interesting."

"Think about it, Dinty," he went on, ripping open a thick, oversized envelope that no doubt contained a manuscript someone wanted him to read. "The first chapter of a book sets everything in motion, starts the dominoes tumbling forward. It is so much easier to see what needs to be there when you've reached an endpoint." He paused here, shrugged. "So really, I just skip the first chapter until I'm done with my first full draft."

I have gone back and forth over the years as to whether Vance meant this literally. Did he really type the words "Chapter Two" on the first page of a new project and start the ball rolling from there?

Or, instead, was he attempting to teach me a lesson by offering a small exaggeration? Perhaps he was really saying, "Don't get stuck in the early stages. Don't think the clumsy paragraphs you write while completing a first draft are even going to be there four drafts later. Don't kid yourself that the first chapter you slave over is even going to end up in the final book."

That's the moral I drew from it, in any case, and it has been useful to me ever since in my writing, whether long-form or short, fiction or memoir. Hundreds of hours of dithering have been avoided by the habit of just getting a few opening sentences down—comprehensible sentences certainly, but not brilliant—and moving forward with my task, secure in the knowledge that I can and will go back and make them better, or more likely replace them, further down the writing road.

If I haven't thanked you before, Vance, I'll do it here: Thanks for that.

So remember, as we discuss opening sentences, opening impulses, opening chapters, and where your story should begin, that the perfect words and sentences don't always show up on the first day. Most likely they won't.

The perfect words and sentences may present themselves only after you've been at it for days, or months, or in some cases years.

This presents you with two choices:

1. Wait for those perfect words. Don't write anything else. Just keep typing and erasing, typing and erasing, until you finally hit the winning numbers in the first sentence lottery, or;

2. Make good use of the time allotted to you. Writing is an act of discovery, and you may need to write some scenes that will appear in the middle of the book, work toward an understanding of your characters, and see through the surface of the story into the further depths, before you can know what the perfect first sentence or page looks like.

Trust the Doctor. Option one is a big mistake. Option two is best.

Beginnings That Work

The beginning of any good story, whether truth or fiction, has one clear goal: put a hook into the reader. Make her lean forward in her chair. Give her a reason to follow along to the second sentence. And then the third.

But if that was the *only* prerequisite, then writing the first sentence would be remarkably easy, and every novel or memoir would begin exactly the same way:

> Dinty winced and whimpered slightly as the very angry person pressed the barrel of the pistol firmly into the side of his head.

You can substitute the name of your main character, or a first person "I," or maybe "the agent who made me wait six months and then sent a one-sentence email saying he would not represent my novel" into that opening instead of my name. You can substitute a knife, blowtorch, or staple gun for the barrel of the pistol. You might make the phrase "very angry person" more precise and descriptive by swapping in "the frustrated author whose genius no one would recognize." But the idea is the same.

Cripes! What happens next?

The reason every novel and memoir does not begin in that fashion, aside from the fact that it would become unbearably tedious, is that the opening, along with setting the hook, must also reflect the deeper story. The *heart* story. The Hero's Journey. The Invisible Magnetic River story. The opening impulse must be intrinsically connected to where your story will go, and thus directly tied to what your character wants most, or fears most, or in some cases is doing her very best to avoid.

Here is the opening sentence of Elizabeth Gilbert's best-selling memoir *Eat, Pray, Love*:

> I wish Giovanni would kiss me.[2]

Some folks just want a glass of water, but Gilbert wants Giovanni, and she wants him bad.

Gilbert's sentence can be taken merely at face value, but if you've read the book, you know that the underlying tension in that sentence goes much further than it seems at first glance. The urge to be kissed by Giovanni connects back to the shattered marriage she is escaping, the loss of love that gobsmacked her and sent her on the journey the book will describe. Moreover, the fact (which we learn later) that Giovanni is younger than Gilbert connects to her worry that she is now far less attractive than her earlier self, and connects also to a brief affair with a young actor named David that came after the dissolution of her marriage, an affair that devastated her even further. And then there is the name: Giovanni. The opening third of the book explores, among other currents of her life, Gilbert's fascination with Italy and the Italian language. The boot-shaped Mediterranean country is not just a spot on the map—it is a metaphor for Gilbert's deeper yearnings.

There is also trouble in that first sentence. Gilbert very early on lets us know that despite the young man's "giant brown liquid-center Italian eyes," being kissed by Giovanni would be a bad thing. Not good for either of them, really.

Gilbert's memoir is subtitled *One Woman's Search for Everything Across Italy, India, and Indonesia.* The words "search for everything" would seem to give the author an enormous amount of latitude as to where she takes us, but in fact, the book is focused and character-driven throughout, from the first sentence on.

Let's look at a few more openings that effectively set up a primal story.

Jodi Picoult's *My Sister's Keeper,* for instance, begins:

> In my first memory, I am three years old and I am trying to kill my sister.[3]

Raymond Chandler's *The Big Sleep* starts with:

> It was about eleven o'clock in the morning, mid October, with the sun not shining and a look of hard wet rain in the clearness of the foothills. I was wearing my powder-blue

suit, with dark blue shirt, tie and display handkerchief, black brogues, black wool socks with dark little clocks on them. I was neat, clean, shaved and sober, and I didn't care who knew it. I was everything the well-dressed private detective ought to be. I was calling on four million dollars.[4]

And Jeffrey Eugenides's *The Virgin Suicides* has this intriguing opening:

On the morning the last Lisbon daughter took her turn at suicide—it was Mary this time, and sleeping pills—the two paramedics arrived at the house knowing exactly where the knife drawer was, and the gas oven, and the beam in the basement from which it was possible to tie a rope.[5]

What all three have in common are questions, intriguing facts, or suggestions compelling the reader to keep turning pages in order to find an explanation. Why does a three-year-old want to kill her sister? Why is Chandler's narrator (the iconic Philip Marlowe) mentioning his sobriety, and only pretending to be "the well-dressed private detective"? The Lisbon daughters are taking turns attempting suicide, and it has gone so far that the paramedics are already familiar with the knife drawer, the oven, the basement beam suited for a noose?

Keep reading.

There are, of course, less lethal ways to accomplish the goal of an effective opening. Tobias Wolff, for instance, begins his memoir, *This Boy's Life*, with the words:

Our car boiled over again just after my mother and I crossed the Continental Divide. While we were waiting for it to cool we heard, from somewhere above us, the bawling of an airhorn. The sound got louder and then a big truck came around the corner and shot past us into the next curve, its trailer shimmying wildly. "Oh, Toby," my mother said, "he's lost his brakes."[6]

No guns, murderous sisters, serial suicides, or disingenuous detectives; just a sense of impending calamity: an engine boiling over, an ominous airhorn, a truck racing past, possibly careening toward the precipice. You should read Wolff's book—it is fantastic—and when you do you will see that his story centers around a marriage that has itself boiled over, and the resulting divorce (Continental Divide) threatens at times to send young Toby and his mother careening off some precipice of their own. Wolff doesn't place a pistol to the side of anyone's skull, but he certainly does set the mood, start the dominoes falling, and hint to the reader that there's plenty of trouble ahead.

Or look at Jane Austen's *Pride and Prejudice* again, as we did in the previous chapter. Austen's novel opens:

> It is a truth universally acknowledged, that a single man in possession of a good fortune, must be in want of a wife. However little known the feelings or views of such a man may be on his first entering a neighbourhood, this truth is so well fixed in the minds of the surrounding families, that he is considered the rightful property of some one or other of their daughters.[7]

The underlying tension, the Invisible River, of *Pride and Prejudice* arises from social norms ("a truth universally acknowledged"), strict gender roles ("must be in want of a wife"), and stern, possibly smothering, expectations ("he is considered the rightful property"). It is all there, in two unassuming opening sentences.

Finally, look at the start of Dickens's *David Copperfield*:

> Whether I shall turn out to be the hero of my own life, or whether that station will be held by anybody else, these pages must show. To begin my life with the beginning of my life, I record that I was born (as I have been informed and believe) on a Friday, at twelve o'clock at night. It was

remarked that the clock began to strike, and I began to cry, simultaneously.[8]

The diction may seem antiquated, but the beginning connects directly to character and journey. A question is posed: will our protagonist become a hero or not? And everything to follow in this classic novel stems directly from that infant's first cry, as young David, and later adult Copperfield, cries out again and again against the injustice of nineteenth-century Britain.

Each of these opening passages has this in common: a promise, and a connection to the deeper story.

Which brings us back to the advice I was given by my mentor Vance Bourjaily. You can't know what belongs in your opening sentence or opening paragraph until you've tracked down your primal story, and sometimes that doesn't happen when you begin your novel or memoir. It can sometimes take weeks or months of exploratory writing, of digging into your imagination or memory, of getting to know what is of the most concern to your main character.

The exploratory writing you need to accomplish might include prewriting about your character, his or her past, and his or her motivations (or exploring your own former self if you are in fact that main character), or it might mean diving right into writing the book, with the understanding that nothing is set in stone, and, as your grasp of the heart story firms up, you may very well be back later to do some important revision.

In the end, just keep breathing and by all means continue writing.

Bad Beginnings

In the *Peanuts* comic strip, Snoopy was often portrayed sitting atop his doghouse, typing away on the opening page of his Great American Novel. In the panel of one strip, the first words of his masterpiece were revealed to be, "It was a dark and stormy night."

Snoopy, the literary beagle, was actually borrowing the opening of *Paul Clifford*, a novel written in 1830 by Sir Edward Bulwer-Lytton.

That novel begins like this:

> It was a dark and stormy night; the rain fell in torrents, except at occasional intervals, when it was checked by a violent gust of wind which swept up the streets (for it is in London that our scene lies), rattling along the housetops, and fiercely agitating the scanty flame of the lamps that struggled against the darkness.[9]

If you've read many nineteenth-century popular novels, this sort of long-winded opening packed with modifiers and qualifiers is not so out of the ordinary. But it feels dated, certainly, and to my ear at least, the phrase "fiercely agitating the scanty flame of the lamps that struggled against the darkness" is a good bit quasi-dramatic—what might be diagnosed as "trying too hard."

In any case, Bulwer-Lytton's dark and stormy opening is often held up as the epitome of bad writing, or purple prose. So much so, that in 1982 the English Department at San Jose State University started the annual Bulwer-Lytton Fiction Contest, a tongue-in-cheek competition whose entrants are invited "to compose the opening sentence to the worst of all possible novels."

The results are often deliberately hilarious.

The truth, however, is that Bulwer-Lytton was quite a successful writer, both popular and well-paid, and within his writings he coined many expressions still in use today—"the great unwashed," "pursuit of the almighty dollar," "the pen is mightier than the sword"—so perhaps he is being unfairly singled out.

Moreover, the brilliant Madeleine L'Engle started her novel *A Wrinkle in Time* with these exact same words:

> It was a dark and stormy night.[10]

She was probably just having some fun with her readers, and, of course, she *did* have the good sense to put a period after the seventh word.

In any case, whether it is dark or stormy where you are sitting right now, or pleasantly warm and sunny, let's wander through the Book Doctor's hypothetical waiting room and explore a few additional ways that openings can go badly awry.

FLORID DESCRIPTION

Readers' expectations and tolerances change over time, and as I mentioned before, there was a period when many British novels did begin with a page or two of description, usually some lovely view of the rural countryside.

Like this:

> A pleasing constellation of snow-tufted sheep scattered across the verdant hillside under the kindly, warmish April sun, alongside a gently burbling brook, filled here and there with multicolored trout, dashing in and out between the firm rocks that lined the solid banks. A few spirited lambs gamboled next to their loving mother ewes, while overhead a wise old hawk swooped and dove through the cerulean expanse of sky. Just over the hill, a charming farmhouse squatted comfortably, with a faint wisp of smoke escaping the noble chimney . . .

Now imagine that going on for two pages.

Then pinch yourself awake.

Perhaps nineteenth-century readers were more tolerant because there were fewer novels (and even fewer memoirs) competing for their attention, and nothing on television, and no cute kitten pictures on the Internet. But if the opening sentences, or one long opening sentence, do little more than set the scene, even if the scene is beautiful, the reader might very well start to think, "I'd be better off going to the museum to look at some paintings."

STIFF DESCRIPTION

If, on the other hand, your opening is not florid at all, but stiff as a marble countertop, you have an entirely different problem.

Read this:

> Jackson Connor was five foot eleven and 180 pounds, with short dark hair and a dark beard. He wore a comfortable sweatshirt, blue denim jeans, and Timberland work boots. He had a large nose, with a freckle just to the left, and blue eyes. He stood next to his 2014 Toyota Camry. His hands were in his pockets.

If the cops were looking for Jackson Connor, they would certainly appreciate the generous and specific detail, but when was the last time you found yourself hopelessly enraptured by a police report?

TORTURED DESCRIPTION

Beware the awkward simile:

> His nose looked like a banana that had been partially straightened out at one end but curved even more than the usual banana at the other.

Was that painful enough?
Okay, here's one more:

> The patient winced when the nurse approached with the needle, like someone who really didn't like having a needle jammed sharply into their arm.

TOO MUCH EXPOSITION

Consider this, dear reader:

> Ever since her brother Billy had dropped dead on the golf
> course, Carolyn Fletcher had been seeing a psychiatrist.
> The doctor told Carolyn that grief was normal when a
> sibling passes but that Carolyn's dangerous new pastime
> was putting her at peril. Carolyn had begun skateboarding
> because she remembered that her brother had loved
> skateboarding when they were children, and though
> Billy hadn't skateboarded for fifty-five years before his
> death, to Carolyn this seemed a fitting way to remember
> him. Carolyn was nearing retirement age, and badly
> overweight. Even climbing steps had become difficult
> as her knees aged. But she was determined. The doctor
> warned that a fall from the skateboard could land Carolyn
> in the emergency room. And the teenage boys at the
> municipal skate park liked to make fun of her, hooting and
> hollering, and calling her "that crazy lady with the death
> wish." Carolyn would not be deterred, however, and had
> even begun listening to hip-hop recording artist Fetty
> Wap, hoping it might help her to fit in . . .

Though sympathetic readers might be a little worried about poor old Carolyn's well-being, the truth is that we never asked to know *everything* about her, right off the bat.

"HIDDEN" EXPOSITION

In this episode, the clever writer takes my warning against too much exposition and turns the exposition into action, if thinking in complete sentences can be truly be called action:

> Carolyn Fletcher sat by her front window, pondering
> what her psychiatrist had told her, that her dangerous
> new pastime of skateboarding in response to her brother

Billy's untimely, golf-related death was putting her at peril. Carolyn recalled that she had begun skateboarding because her brother had loved skateboarding when they were children, and though Billy hadn't skateboarded for fifty-five years before his death, to Carolyn this seemed like a fitting way to remember him. Carolyn chuckled inwardly, remembering that the kindly psychiatrist had pointed out that she was nearing retirement age, and was badly overweight, and that Fetty Wap's lyrics were shockingly obscene . . .

It turns out Carolyn thinks *a lot* about herself, and readers fall asleep, *a lot.*

THE MEMOIR OVERSELL

As in:

> My brothers and sisters were the goofiest cast of characters you could ever meet, truly a laugh a minute, and believe me, there was never a dull moment in the Hurley household . . .

Or:

> My ex-husband, Tom, was the biggest bastard ever to have walked the face of the planet . . .

Or:

> This is a story of redemption, of how I took the foulest circumstances anyone could imagine and found a way to turn tears of sorrow into tears of joy. It worked for me, and it could work for you too!!

Advice from the Book Doctor: *Just tell the story, dammit.*

THE ALARM CLOCK PLOY

> Roland Lemay was being chased through the unlit alley by four large, dark figures, howling and snorting like wolves, and the faster Roland ran, the faster they pursued, until he turned into a side alley and saw a fence blocking his path. "I'm going to die," Roland cried out to no one, and the lupine figures quickly gathered at his back, pulled him roughly to the ground. "This is it," he thought, "my final moment on Earth." Then there was a loud ringing, and Roland started, realizing that he was in bed, dreaming it all. "That's the last time I eat an entire mushroom and bacon pizza just before turning in for the night," he chuckled to himself.

So Roland is safe after all, but unfortunately not everyone is safe, because it is at this point that the reader pulls out a gun, and shoots the author at point-blank range.

THE HARD-BOILED DETECTIVE

Crime novels have their specific joys and attractions, and their own very specific clichés:

> Philip Logan rubbed the side of his temple, nursing the worst hangover of his life, and glared into the bright Los Angeles sunlight, scanning the bleak landscape for any sign of a tavern, where he could get a stiff shot of cheap bourbon, just to take the edge off the headache that was threatening to shatter his brain into a million little pieces . . .

All of the genres—science fiction, romance, fantasy, western, you name it—have similar openings that might have been done once to great effect, that may have been reprised another time or two without any great harm coming to the writer, but that have become so familiar as to be laughable.

Avoid them.

Like the plague.

Or any other cliché.

So, how do we avoid falling into these traps?

Actually, you probably will fall into them.

The "clichéd opening" pitfall is so very easy to fall into, simply because clichéd phrases and approaches are often the first that come to mind. They are all too familiar and thus effortlessly summoned.

But that's why your keyboard has a delete key.

THE INFORMATION DUMP

The other main category of bad beginnings is the the urge to give the reader *all* of the backstory—on your character, or on yourself as memoirist—right up front, so that everything that follows will make perfect sense.

Well, you needn't make perfect sense, or explain yourself or your character, right away—readers are more than happy to put up with a little mystery, as long as they feel that they are in the hands of an author who will remember to dot the i's and cross the t's eventually.

When you meet someone in real life whom you find immediately intriguing, is it because you know *everything* about them already?

I suspect not. More likely, you know just enough to be curious.

In the end, it is a delicate balance you are seeking. You want the reader to have questions, to want to read forward in the chapter, and ultimately in the book, but you don't want to leave them too much in the dark. So give a little, just enough to start the character down her path, and drop the rest of the needed information along the way, like bread crumbs, or snow-tufted sheep scattered across a verdant hillside.

Beginning at the End

But what about outlining your novel or memoir? If you plan the whole book out ahead of time, you will know exactly where to begin, won't you?

There are two schools of thought on this, and frankly, neither is wrong.

A few writers—and in my experience, they form the smaller of the two groups—are able to see their novel or memoir's path all the way through from the beginning, and are able to roughly outline—sometimes intricately outline—where it begins, where it ends, and what goes in every chapter.

To be honest, I'm a fair bit jealous of those writers for whom this technique works. I imagine they have fewer crises of faith, not quite so many late-night attacks of the "I can't ever finish this book, it is beyond me" variety.

Maybe not.

For me, though, and for many writers I've talked with, a writing project of any depth and length can't be mapped out ahead of time, because writing is essentially an act of discovery. If you put the main character of your novel in a situation, an interesting predicament, it is through writing scenes and taking that character from moment to moment and place to place that you discover what happens, how he meets the challenge, and what ultimately results as the story spools out.

Even in a memoir, where you are writing from memory, and thus you know what actually occurred, the book still is fueled by questions:

- Why did this happen?

- What could my parents possibly have been thinking?

- Why did Aunt Calista stop speaking with everyone else in our family?

- What did that year of living in a small Zambian village teach me about the world?

Writing the memoir is how you discover your answers—a process of thinking aloud on the page, of uncovering what you didn't know the morning you sat down to begin your book.

Even if you know exactly what occurred, and on what day and what precise time, the human animal is a mystery, and why people acted certain ways, what they hid from you, what you hid from others, what you may remember only thinly, what you are pretty sure you don't remember at all, and how all of this gathered together to shape who you are at forty or seventy-five, combines to make the engine of a memoir.

The book, in other words, is not just about what happened. It is about what you make of it now.

In my opinion, and my experience, a writer who hopes to create something fresh and lasting does not sit down at the typewriter or keyboard and just say what he or she wants to say. She sits down with questions, sees where they lead her, discovers new questions, and follows them into unexpected territory.

A few writers can do this even with an outline in place. For most of us, though, outlining and knowing what is going to occur at every point along the way results in a stiff book, one with a character who seems pushed and pulled from chapter to chapter, rather than one in which the character seems alive, complex, and, like real human beings, often a bit contradictory.

In memoir you risk a narrator who is perhaps trying too hard to teach a lesson, or one who is forcing a foregone conclusion, rather than a human narrator open to serendipity and surprise.

I said at the outset that neither side in the should-I-outline-my-book debate is wrong. What is necessary, then, is discovering what works best for you.

And now that I think about it, my process actually falls somewhere in the middle. I stop and scribble rough outlines of my book-in-progress many times over the year or so that I'm working on it. And a week later I throw the latest outline away, and I conjure up a new one. The book itself reminds me again and again where it wants to travel.

What Is *Your* Beginning?

Wouldn't it be great if I could just tell you where to begin? Wouldn't it be fantastic if I could easily answer the question of where to begin, not just for you but for aspiring writers everywhere? Heck, I'd be unbelievably wealthy, just like a real doctor.

But I'm going to have to wait for my country club member-ship and white Cadillac, because the honest answer is that you can find the right place to begin only when you are deep in the process of writing, by coming to a more complex understanding of your characters (real or fictional), what they desire and what they fear, and by listening as your book speaks back to you.

In fiction, the characters, when I find myself deep into a scene or chapter, will say something unexpected in the dialogue, or will react to another character in ways that surprise me. It's uncanny, actually. I know it is me who just typed the words, but for a moment the words startle me, as if my fingers had a mind of their own.

No, the Book Doctor didn't just steal happy pills from his own prescription cabinet. When my writing is at its best, it *really does* talk back to me.

In memoir, too. Even as I write about my own life, the life I know best, forward and backward, I find myself writing something I didn't know I knew. Maybe some fresh understanding of how the world looked from my mother's perspective, or perhaps some new insight into why I made such perilous choices during my early twenties. And then, when I see it there on the page, I realize something new about the book I am writing, some fresh facet or direction.

Or maybe I don't actually type the words, but an idea pops into my head as I step from the shower, and I write it down on a scrap of paper, and later it turns out to be a solution to some area of the book where I'd been stuck for days, writing hopelessly dull sentences or spinning my wheels in mute silence.

The answers are often not in my head but (metaphorically at least) at the tip of my fingers as I type.

But *your* beginning?

I prescribe trial and error, cutting and pasting, a heavy dose of the delete key, and lots of trying again.

Just remember that the opening sentences must do two things:

1. Give the reader a reason (an honest reason, not a gimmick) to keep reading.
2. Resonate with the primal, heart story. Your opening might present the situation directly—"I wish Giovanni would kiss me"—or indirectly—"It is a truth universally acknowledged, that a single man in possession of a good fortune, must be in want of a wife"—or it might be delivered by use of an image—the truck hurtling past young Toby and his mother—but it has to start the Invisible Magnetic River immediately flowing downstream, toward the distant but inevitable end.

⊞ THE BOOK DOCTOR MAKES A HOUSE CALL

The Cure for False Starts and Dull Beginnings

Every writer makes mistakes. Bad writers leave them in place. Successful writers return to the scene of the crime and clean them up.

❶ DIAGNOSIS: You Just Can't Find the Opening Sentence

Well, perhaps I've answered this one already, out in the waiting room. But doctors like to repeat themselves, so here it is again.

▰▱> THE CURE

Don't know how your book should open?

You just don't know y*et*, so keep writing.

▰▱> AN ALTERNATE CURE

Put a bad sentence in place, trusting that you will come back and revise it later.

❶ DIAGNOSIS: You Can't Part with Your Lovely Description

It is all too easy to fall in love with our own writing, especially if we've spent hours or even days crafting and recrafting the descriptive passage. The prospect of having to cut the hard-earned sentences or paragraphs, of perhaps having wasted those hours or days, is a tough pill to swallow.

Opening with description that doesn't immediately jump-start your story—no matter how lovely the writing—is almost always a mistake, however.

Do you want your readers' first thought to be: "Why exactly is he telling me all of this?"

If the descriptive passage *is* lovely, save it, and find a place for it later in the book.

Remember, we don't need to see the entire landscape of your grandparents' farm right away. We probably don't need to see it until we reach that point in the memoir where you step down your Pap-Pap's back kitchen steps and walk out to throw some scraps to the hogs. Show us then. Let us see all of it through the eyes of the nine-year-old you.

We don't need to learn your character's entire backstory, either, no matter how compellingly written, until you've given us a reason to care about your character. Or as Isaac Bashevis Singer has said, "When a writer tries to explain too much . . . he's out of time before he begins."[11]

So tell us only what we need to know.

And even then, scatter it around.

Keep the story moving.

❶ DIAGNOSIS: All the Good Stuff Comes Later

Unless your first name happens to be Stephen and your last name happens to be King, and you are *that* Stephen King, readers are never going to get to all of the wonderfully absorbing material that comes in chapter two if chapter one leaves them yawning, indifferent, or confused.

I'm not criticizing Stephen King here, by the way. He writes tremendous openings. I'm just pointing out that if you've earned a loyal audience of millions based on your earlier books, a reader might be more patient. But if you are trying to pull readers into your *first* book, you need to make sure the story magnet is very strong.

And to be practical for a moment, there won't be *any* readers yawning indifferently at your chapter one if your opening pages aren't working to create curiosity and interest, because agents and editors are the toughest readers out there, and if your opening pages don't get past them, your book likely won't ever see the light of day.

THE CURE

Start with action, character, and your best writing.

 ## PROMPTS AND EXERCISES TO CURE STORY PROBLEMS

Trial and error are a writer's best friends. Try these opening moves on for size.

SPEAKING OF STEPHEN KING

King has his own theories on the importance of a novel's introductory sentence:

> An opening line should invite the reader to begin the story. It should say: Listen. Come in here. You want to know about this.[12]

Chart where your opening lines actually invite the reader in. What are you offering: mystery, humor, lively characterization, a compelling question (stated or unstated)? What is it the reader is going to immediately want to know? What does your opening suggest a reader should listen most closely for in the coming pages?

Read your first sentence, and then your first page, as if you hadn't written any of it yourself, as if you had just run across these words written by a stranger, and ask yourself, *Would I keep reading?*

And if so, *Why?*

LET'S IMPROVISE

There is no one way a book begins, so let's try many ways, a myriad of approaches, a virtual medicine cabinet of ideas.

Try improvising a first sentence for the book you are writing, based on these openings from published writers:

William Least Heat-Moon, begins *Blue Highways* with a warning: "Beware thoughts that come in the night."[13]

What warning would fit at the beginning of your book?

Beware _____

_____.

Mary Karr opens her memoir *The Liars' Club* with a significant early memory: "My sharpest memory is of a single instant surrounded by dark."[14]

What is your sharpest early memory, or that of your main character?

_____

_____.

J. D. Salinger's *The Catcher in the Rye* starts us off with an irreverent, informal introductory evasion of a sentence: "If you really want to hear about it, the first thing you'll probably want to know is where I was born, and what my lousy childhood was like, and how my parents were occupied and all before they had me, and all that David Copperfield kind of crap, but I don't feel like going into it, if you want to know the truth."[15]

Try the same, for yourself or your character:

If you really want to hear about it, the first thing you'll probably want to know is _____ but I don't feel like going into it . . .

Albert Camus opens *The Stranger* with just three words: "Mother died today."[16]

What three-word opening would start the ball rolling in your book?

_____.

F. Scott Fitzgerald's *The Great Gatsby* teases the reader's curiosity by referencing a parent's early guidance: "In my younger and more vulnerable years my father gave me some advice that I've been turning over in my mind ever since."[17]

If that were your first line (feel free to swap out father and insert mother, grandmother, teacher, pet turtle, or whatever works), what would be in the second sentence, hinting further at the tidbit of remembered advice?

_____

_____

Rafael Sabatini opens *Scaramouche* with a broad, colorful description: "He was born with a gift of laughter and a sense that the world was mad."[18]

Do the same for your novel's main character:

(S)he was born with _____

_____

Or for your memoir:

I was born with _____

_____

Feel free to mimic the openings of books that you love.

The more you try, the more you will see the infinite possibilities.

"Plot springs from character. . . . I've always sort of believed that these people inside me—these characters—know who they are and what they're about and what happens, and they need me to help get it down on paper because they don't type."

—ANNE LAMOTT[1]

3 | PRESCRIPTIONS FOR HEALTHY PROSE

CHARACTER, DIALOGUE, AND SETTING

This chapter will cover a lot of ground—not unlike your annual checkup, perhaps—but hopefully this checkup will be far less embarrassing.

For instance, you needn't exchange your clothes for a flimsy hospital "gown" before this doctor comes in.

And I won't be commenting on the weight you've gained.

Instead, we'll examine *character*, *dialogue*, and *setting*, and how a healthy dose of each will keep your book manuscript fit and trim.

Character as Story

Character *is* story.

The stories we tell and retell—whether those we trade with friends over lunch or those we write into novels and memoirs—are inevitably about people, our strengths and weaknesses, our better moments and wretched failures. The human story is what holds our interest. That's where story begins and ends.

Even in children's books, where the story might feature a baby panda, a runaway bunny, or Ferdinand the Bull, the panda, the bunny, and Ferdinand are personified—imbued with human yearnings. Other genres—interplanetary science fiction, or fantasy tales filled with elves and ogres—also use human behavior as the model for their nonhuman characters. Think of the robots R2-D2 or C-3PO in the *Star Wars* movies: their human side is what brings the drama, or comedy.

Though novels often tackle broad subjects, the human experiences at the center are, again, what make them memorable. *The Grapes of Wrath*, for instance, though valuable for its depiction of the Great Depression and the ravages of drought, ultimately focuses on the Joads, a poor family of tenant farmers. Without the Joads, and their stories, *The Grapes of Wrath* would be a history textbook, an economic treatise, or a mere list of bleak statistics.

Memoir, of course, focuses on human experience too. In this instance, your characters are real people—you, the author, and the folks you have known and seen—but characters nonetheless (once you decide to put them in your book).

So how does character work in story?

The first principle I need to share, and the one that sometimes seems hardest for beginning writers to grasp, is that it is not your job to *define* your character. Your character's actions, reactions, and lack of action, along with his words and silences, will define him for the reader far more effectively and believably than anything you have to say on the subject.

Your job is not to define the character, but to help readers visualize him, in depth, with all the contradiction and complexity of a real human being.

For instance, consider this sentence:

> Bob was insensitive and caustic.

Those are just words. Abstract words. We as readers can define them, but we don't see them, or feel them. They register in our brain, not in our nervous system.

Instead:

> Bob barely looked at the young waiter who brought the massive porterhouse to his corner table. "There better be no pink in the center," he barked, waving the steak knife

perilously close to his girlfriend Danielle's left arm,
"or you'll be going home with no tip."

Most readers will have an emotional reaction to this second example. If you've ever earned your living waiting on tables, as I have, I'm guessing that reaction will be fairly strong.

So why does it work this way? To understand, think of how you come to know people in real life.

Let's say it is just past midnight, and your sister Tina, the one who has hasn't always shown the best judgment in men, calls you on your cell phone, announcing, "I've met this guy. His name is Rich. I'm inviting him to Mom and Dad's for Thanksgiving dinner. He's such a sweetheart. I know you're all going to like Rich a lot!"

What goes through your mind?

The normal human response, aside from being annoyed at your sister for calling so late, is to think to yourself something along these lines: "I'll believe it when I see it."

That's what thinking people do: they register an idea, and then wait to see proof before accepting the idea as solid fact.

If Thanksgiving rolls around, and Rich shows up for dinner two hours late, in plaid shorts and a dirty T-shirt, reeking of cheap bourbon, greeting your mom with the words "Hey pretty mama, when do we chow down?" in a grating voice, you'll suspect your sister has made yet another lousy relationship decision.

If he rips the drumstick off the turkey with his bare hands and repeatedly casts aspersions on your Aunt Lucy's holiday sweater, you'll be convinced.

If, on the other hand, Rich shows up with flowers for the hostess, pets the dog, makes your five-year-old niece giggle with his silly faces, and mentions that he has a steady job, you're ready to start believing your sister has done all right for once. If he helps to wash the dishes, you'll be sold.

We believe it only when we see it for ourselves.

Well, this same rule applies to the printed page. You can tell the reader "Rich is such a sweetheart," or "Bob was insensitive and caustic," as many times as you want, but the reader won't be convinced until the reader is able to make his or her own appraisal.

That appraisal is only possible, however, if you put Bob down on the page, and let him walk, talk, bark, and wave his steak knife perilously close to his girlfriend's left arm, showing himself for exactly who he is.

In addition to sometimes forgetting the importance of *demonstrating* attributes like sweetness or rudeness, the beginning writer often fails to draw a full physical portrait of a character, denying readers the chance to see an actual, flesh-and-blood person, to know how she walks across a room, to see what she does with her hands when nervous or upset, or to hear her particular speech inflections.

This is so easy to forget, because you, the author, can see your characters in great detail. After all, they live somewhere in your head. Thus when you read a sentence you've written—"Danielle shifted her chair away from Bob, gently lifted her gin and tonic from the table, and poured it slowly into Bob's lap"—you are seeing a woman of a particular height, with an exact hairstyle, wearing a distinctive blouse, and glaring at her rude boyfriend in a specific way.

You see all of this because you have spent so many hours picturing Danielle in your mind as you went through the first, second, and third draft of the book.

But if *we* can't see her, Danielle does not exist.

This is true in fiction writing, and it is true, of course, in memoir, because in memoir you are quite often picturing someone you have known for years, or perhaps for your whole life. Keep in mind that whether you are writing about your mother, your neighbor, a Tuscan fig farmer, or yourself, the fact that your reader has never met any of these folks means that you will need to build these individuals trait by trait just as a novelist builds imaginary characters.

And finally, where character is concerned, remember all that we discussed about primal story, the Invisible Magnetic River, and how your characters' yearnings, fears, and worries are what begins the tumbling of the dominoes on page one. In a book that covers months or years of the character's life, moreover, remember that yearnings, fears, and worries are not static; they change, transform, disappear, reappear, and essentially shape the lives that we lead.

A flat cardboard character acts just one way, and wants just one thing.

Real humans are far more complicated.

Dialogue as Story

Dialogue tells a story too: not so much the story of who we are as the story of how we choose to present ourselves.

Unless you've taken a truth serum (and there is little agreement as to whether these serums even work), what you say on any given day is a mixture of the truth, what you think is true but actually isn't, what you want others to think you think is true even though you don't truly believe it, deliberate evasion, forgetfulness, and outright lies.

I'm not accusing you of being unreliable. I am accusing you of being human.

Yet despite the capriciousness of speech, we human beings remain spellbound by the words of others. How often have you heard people asking these questions:

> "What did he say, *really*?"
> "So how did she wriggle out of *that* one?"
> "She expects me to believe *what*?"

Just as character is not a flat piece of cardboard—Grandmom is kind, and that's all there is to it—what we say and how we say it are not as simple as the dictionary definitions of the words we speak.

Compare these two examples:

> "Why did you cheat on me?" my wife demands to know.
>
> "I had a moment of weakness," I answer, "and I am so sorry for what I did. To be honest, I can't fully explain my actions. And now, as we stand here looking one another in the eye, I deeply hope this isn't going to destroy your trust in me."

Pretty clear, but also horribly flat.

People don't often speak in complete sentences, for one thing, and we seldom answer a question straightforwardly, certainly not when we've done something we badly regret.

Compare this longer exchange:

> I drop my keys on the front table, walk to the kitchen, and ask Stacy how her day has been. She doesn't answer. I tell her my day has basically been a waste. She still doesn't answer. I point out to her that she's not saying anything.
>
> She narrows her eyes and leans against the center island. "Tell me why you did it, Patrick."
>
> "Did what?" I ask.
>
> "You know what I'm talking about."
>
> "I have no idea."
>
> She thinks about that for maybe two seconds before she asks the logical question. "You have no idea why you did it, or no idea what I'm talking about?"
>
> "Why I did it."
>
> Stacy turns her back and opens the door of the refrigerator, leaving me to think about this stupid thing I've done. This very stupid thing. A minute later she has

a glass of wine in her hand—just one glass, not two—and exits into the living room, where she sits down in the oversized armchair.

I follow.

"What were you trying to do?" she asks. "Hurt me?"

"No," I say, standing across the room. "It had nothing to do with you."

She blinks and sips. I take a few steps in and lower myself into a chair as well, thinking about how idiotic my last comment just sounded. She's my wife. How could this not be about her?

After a while, I try talking again.

"We went out after work with some people from the office. She missed her ride. I offered to drive her home. She asked me in."

"She asked you in?"

"Right. And it just sort of happened."

"Just sort of happened?" Stacy is almost smiling, but not because she's happy, or because she's ready to forgive. Perhaps she just likes seeing me swing in the wind.

"I'm not proud of this," I say. "I screwed up."

Her eyebrows lift. "Really?"

Neither person in this fictional marriage is saying exactly what is in their mind, and neither one of them is willing to be fully vulnerable. They are doing what real people do: talking around the subject, parsing words, employing sarcasm, answering questions with other questions, dodging the direct response.

Yet a reader can learn a good bit about Patrick and Stacy through this exchange, by interpreting the nuance of their language, the pauses, the reasons behind the evasive answers, and, of course, Stacy's body language and the choreography as they move from room to room.

In other words, the readers have to figure it out for themselves (with the material provided by a careful author). In fact, they very much want to figure it out for themselves.

That's one of the joys of reading.

Putting two and two together and reaching our own determination is an engaging and welcome challenge for readers, and since we are the ones making the determination, what we eventually decide about these characters seems all the more real and true.

Two last thoughts on dialogue:

Notice that the preceding exchange doesn't feature adverbs, as in "Stacey said sarcastically" or "I answered meekly." If the character's intentions are not clear from the words and context, you need to go back and work on the words and context.

Even the verbs themselves may be unnecessary, Elmore Leonard reminds us: "The line of dialogue belongs to the character; the verb is the writer sticking his nose in."[2]

Keep your nose out of it.

But use your ears.

The best way to capture the rhythm and irregularity of real speech is to listen to people talking, listen to what is behind the words, and hear how often we interrupt one another and how often we interrupt ourselves. Take note of how often we ignore a question, or answer the question with another question. Notice just how messy our speech is, how full of sentence fragments and unfinished thoughts.

"If you are using dialogue—say it aloud as you write it," the great John Steinbeck advised. "Only then will it have the sound of speech."[3]

Setting as Story

Lives do not occur in a vacuum, and the moments we choose to explore (in fiction or memoir) must occur somewhere, tangible and real.

Setting is integral to story, because the places we choose to be (or are stuck with because we have no alternative), and the things we choose to surround ourselves with (or are stuck with because we can't afford what we really want), and the endless small details of the spaces we construct for ourselves reveal much about the deeper person we (or our characters) are.

Moreover, how our characters interact with these spaces offers yet another way for readers to determine who our characters are and to come to an understanding of our characters' fears and yearnings, hopes and dreams, strengths and weaknesses.

Here is an example of setting as story from Charles Dickens in his short novel *A Christmas Carol*:

> The door of Scrooge's counting-house was open that he might keep his eye upon his clerk, who in a dismal little cell beyond, a sort of tank, was copying letters. Scrooge had a very small fire, but the clerk's fire was so very much smaller that it looked like one coal. But he couldn't replenish it, for Scrooge kept the coal-box in his own room; and so surely as the clerk came in with the shovel, the master predicted that it would be necessary for them to part. Wherefore the clerk put on his white comforter, and tried to warm himself at the candle; in which effort, not being a man of a strong imagination, he failed.[4]

Scrooge, of course, is a tightwad—so stingy with a dollar that his name has now become shorthand for miserly behavior—and his office reflects his character precisely.

Here is another example, from F. Scott Fitzgerald's *The Great Gatsby*:

> We walked through a high hallway into a bright rosy-colored space, fragilely bound into the house by French windows at either end. The windows were ajar and gleaming white against the fresh grass outside that seemed to grow a little way into the house. A breeze blew through the room, blew curtains in at one end and out the other like pale flags, twisting them up toward the frosted wedding-cake of the ceiling, and then rippled over the wine-colored rug, making a shadow on it as wind does on the sea.
>
> The only completely stationary object in the room was an enormous couch on which two young women were buoyed up as though upon an anchored balloon. They were both in white, and their dresses were rippling and fluttering as if they had just been blown back in after a short flight around the house. I must have stood for a few moments listening to the whip and snap of the curtains and the groan of a picture on the wall. Then there was a boom as Tom Buchanan shut the rear windows and the caught wind died out about the room and the two young women ballooned slowly to the floor.[5]

There is a lot going on in those two descriptive paragraphs, including a glimpse of the extreme wealth and privilege to be found in the mansion overlooking the Manhasset Bay. Fitzgerald is setting the mood here, while also subtly suggesting that whatever lightness there is in this house comes from outside, carried by the breeze. What lies inside, once the window closes, is perhaps more ominous.

Though both of these examples demonstrate well the interrelationship of setting and story, let me point out that not every description of place needs to be so obviously reflective of a character's major trait (Scrooge's parsimonious soul mirrored by his bleak counting-house) or so deeply symbolic (the two young women ballooning to the floor).

Every knickknack on every shelf needn't be imbued with deep significance—that, in fact, can itself get tedious and overwrought.

Sometimes the details of room and house and landscape are just there to make the story seem real. Setting—not unlike some minor peculiarities of speech or gesture, or the clothing a character wears, or the style of a character's hair—can be important to your novel or memoir for the simple reason that it allows the reader to feel that these are real people, living real lives, in actual physical spaces, and in that way the reader can begin to care about the character, want to follow the story.

Unless you were deliberately launching an experimental theatrical experience, you wouldn't put your actors out on the stage without clothing, without a table to set the props down upon, without a chair, and for that matter, without a painted backdrop showing the time period and style of the drawing room where the action occurs.

An audience wants to see the play, and the action, occurring *somewhere*, and so do readers.

✚ THE BOOK DOCTOR MAKES A HOUSE CALL
The Cure for Common Character, Dialogue, and Setting Problems

Locating the details that create memorable characters and setting can be time-consuming, but it is time well spent. The best books allow readers to forget for the moment that they are reading, to feel as if they are actually there, in the world of the book, experiencing every turn. The intimate details of character and setting are what make that possible.

❶ DIAGNOSIS: You've Established Your Character (By Showing Him Acting with Extreme Rudeness Toward the Waiter), So What Now?

If the only trait you can think of to describe your character—or your ex-husband—is that he is rude to waiters, you need to go back and work on character some more (and ask yourself why you married the guy in the first place).

Real people are full of contradictions, and so are good characters, in a novel or memoir.

➤ THE CURE

Explore those contradictions.

But not all at once. Incrementally. As it happens in real life.

When someone new enters your world, as a friend, a fellow worker, a boyfriend to your younger sister, how do you decide what sort of person they are and what you think of them? Does this process play out as they stand absolutely still, about six feet away from you, and you study them for five minutes?

No. We come to understand and form our feelings toward people based on their words and actions *over time*.

So in your book, let the picture become clearer (but also more complex, because that's how real people are in the world) as each chapter advances.

❶ DIAGNOSIS: You Can't Remember What Your Aunt Ethel Was Wearing When She Fell Out of the Boat

This is a common concern of memoirists. If we are writing about events that happened twenty years ago, how can we possibly remember dialogue accurately or small details like clothing and weather?

In truth, if you are writing about something that happened twenty *minutes* ago, memory is such that absolute accuracy is unlikely. It seems the very moment something happens, we begin forgetting bits and pieces.

Yet dialogue and description are essential to creating character, to letting the reader sense who people are and how they act. Dialogue allows us as readers to see firsthand, and thus believe what we see, rather than relying on the author to explain it to us.

So what to do?

▬▷ THE CURE

If the moment you are writing about is an important turning point in your past—the day your mother came and took you out of school before lunch to tell you she was divorcing your father, or the moment your parents sat you down and told you that your baby sister was seriously ill and might not survive, or your own cancer diagnosis at age thirty—memory is often quite strong. These moments are often seared into our consciousness, such that they can be recalled with startling accuracy.

But what about those moments not easily recalled?

Well, you probably remember, with some effort, more than you think you do. Picture your memory as a thick rope extending deep into a well, down into the darkness where it is nearly impossible to see. Pull on the rope, and memories will be pulled up as well—*Oh, right, Aunt Ethel always wore that bright orange life jacket, two sizes too big for her.* The new recollection will often, if you sit with it and picture it vividly in your mind, trigger a second memory (the modest blue-striped bathing suit under the life vest), and then a third (the words your father would use when he teased Aunt Ethel, his sister, about how pale she was, and the look on her face when he did this).

Sometimes memory can be researched. You might, for instance, ask others who were there what they remember. You might look for photographs from the time, either family photos or even the photos of strangers that record details of place, of clothing, of hairstyles. What was on television in August 1973? What would have been the headline in your local newspaper? Look at grocery store advertisements. Research what would have been playing on the radio.

By the way, don't let the fact that your cousins remember that day in the boat differently than you remember it put you off. *Your* memory, if it still seems right to you after questioning it and hearing other versions, is the one that matters in your memoir (with the caveat that comes next).

Here's the caveat: *You know when you are flat-out lying.*

Don't do that. Don't say your sister pushed your brother out of the boat and he almost drowned, if that never happened. (Or keep the imagined detail, and write your story as fiction.)

You know also when you are exaggerating wildly to make it funnier or more horrific. Don't do that either.

On the other hand, where smaller, textural details are concerned, like snippets of dialogue or clothing, sophisticated readers understand that all a memoirist has to offer is his or her best-faith effort. So give the reader your very best. If you doubt the accuracy of a memory, let the reader know. If you and your sister have polar opposite takes on that Christmas Eve argument, the reasons you see it differently might be as interesting as the fight itself, so explore that with the reader. Digging through memory is a journey of sorts, so it is often quite appropriate to bring the reader along, through clarity and fog.

Maybe your father didn't use those exact words, but he talked like that. He made that sort of joke. Maybe your mother wore that yellow sweater over her blue dress that day, or maybe it was the day before, and you've mixed the two up. But that is how she dressed.

In the end, if you've thought hard about your memory, explored it, checked it where possible, and it seems accurate, write it down. The reader understands how memory works, and asks only that you share honestly what your memory can bring back, what it can pull up to the surface.

This is the best you can do, so keep writing.

❶ DIAGNOSIS: Your Story Doesn't Happen Anywhere Special

Herman Melville set his novel on a whaling ship. That's hard to beat.

But here's the good news: you don't have to.

➤ THE CURE

We don't need pristine sand and clear blue waters. We don't need rolling moors dotted with pale purple heather. We don't need majestic pines and breathtaking mountain peaks.

Setting might be as simple as the inside of a mobile home, if that is where your main character, or your grandmother, spends most of her time. The old brown sofa that has patches sewn on the arms is setting. The empty lot across the street is setting. The refrigerator that hums too loudly is setting.

What is important is that your story happens in a place, and that the reader can see it, including the little details that make any place unique.

With memoir, just describe what was there.

In fiction, don't try too hard to invent "dramatic" settings. The real world is plenty interesting.

PROMPTS AND EXERCISES TO CURE CHARACTER, DIALOGUE, AND SETTING PROBLEMS

Once you've got your first chapter, gather your colored pens and pencils, and your sense of play; we're going to explore some of the finer points of character, dialogue, and setting.

THE GREEN, PINK, YELLOW OF CHARACTER

Grab a handful of highlighters, in different colors.

Now grab your first chapter.

Read it out loud to yourself—slowly—and highlight (in yellow, let's say) every instance where you *tell* the reader what to believe about a character:

> Millie is fussy.

Then, in pink, highlight every instance where you *show* the reader some aspect of the character's personality:

> Millie's books were arranged alphabetically, all of the spines lined up precisely at shelf's edge.

Finally, in green, highlight every instance where *we see your character in action*, moving through space and time, revealing personality along the way:

> Millie bustled her way into the church basement and immediately began rearranging the plastic silverware on the long tables. "No, no," she muttered. "These are all wrong." When Maggie Miller came out of the kitchen and pointed out that an all-you-can-eat fried fish dinner on paper plates was not exactly a formal occasion, Millie didn't even look up. "Proper etiquette is appropriate

for any occasion," she snapped, still switching forks and knives from left to right. "Now make yourself useful and help me refold these napkins."

If your chapter has much more green than pink, and little or no yellow, you are on the right track.

If not, take your medicine and get back to work.

INFERTILE DIALOGUE

Read the dialogue that follows:

> Tommy walks into the break room, coffee cup in hand.
> "Hey Tommy," Sarah says brightly.
> "Hey Sarah."
> "How are you?"
> "Oh, I'm pretty good."
> "That's great to hear. How's your wife, Melinda?"
> Tommy hesitates a moment. "She's not doing too well."
> "Oh, I'm so sorry. What's wrong?"
> "Well, Sarah, we are trying to have a baby, as I might have told you sometime last year, but we've been trying for over eight months and Melinda is not yet pregnant. My wife is understandably worried about whether we will ever be able to become pregnant, and I am as well. I had a test, of course, just last month, and the doctor found no abnormality with my sperm count. Melinda has been checked out too, by her own doctor, and that doctor likewise found no root cause for why our pregnancy plans haven't come to fruition. We try to remain optimistic, but the longer this goes on, the harder it is to feel confident. Do you know that according to the US Centers for Disease Control and Prevention, 6.7 million women between the ages of fifteen and forty-four suffer from impaired fecundity?"

Now take a deep breath.

If you'd like to step away a moment to Google the phrase "impaired fecundity," feel free to do so.

But whatever fecundity means, this is not how real people talk. So for this exercise, try your hand at rewriting this scene.

First, eliminate what isn't necessary. "Hey Tommy," tells us nothing about our characters, the situation, or the story. Likewise, "Hey Sarah," shows us zilch. In fact, assuming the heart of this scene and story connects to the young couple's problems with conception, we don't need the first seven lines at all. Let Sarah see something on Tommy's face that prompts her to ask, "What's wrong?" Or perhaps he takes a magazine sitting on the break table, one with an infant's cute face beaming out, and turns it over so the cover can't be seen.

What can you come up with to make this exchange start precisely when it begins to press on the nerve of the moment?

After eliminating what doesn't add substance, what we are left with is Tommy's long speech, albeit wholly unbelievable, because no one talks that way, without interruption, especially when the subject is intimate and, for many, uncomfortable.

Rewrite the speech, so it isn't a speech at all but an interaction. How might a thirty-two-year-old man working in an office setting talk to a trusted coworker in a break room about his wife's infertility and depression?

Would Sarah just sit there? (Actually, is she sitting, or standing, walking around the room, or doing a yoga pose? We aren't given any indication.)

Does she reassure Tommy along the way, offer him encouragement to keep unburdening himself, or does the subject make her uncomfortable as well?

What words would Tommy use to explain such an intimate problem? Where would he pause, trail off, or think twice before continuing? What would he leave unsaid?

And if he did indeed walk into the break room with a coffee cup in hand, he must be there because he wants a refill. So, has he already poured his coffee? Is the conversation happening while he fills his cup? Did the last person leave the pot empty, meaning Tommy is making a new pot at the same time that he fills his friend Sarah in on what's happening in his marriage?

There is no correct answer to those questions, except that Tommy should be doing something.

And Sarah too. If she's sitting at the table, is she eating, or reading the newspaper?

Are they alone, or is Tommy having to speak softly, to maintain some privacy?

Is there a window in the break room? A vending machine? A microwave?

Is the room sterile and cold or comfortable and inviting, and what details make it so?

You get the idea. We need a full picture: dialogue, character, setting, and action.

When you're done charting how you might handle a scene like the stiff, unbelievable one I've provided, look back at your own dialogue-heavy moments. Do you see anything you can improve?

THE HEARTBEAT OF PLACE

In his excellent book *The Art of Fiction*, novelist John Gardner offers up an exercise on setting that has become one of those most often used in classrooms and by individual writers trying to better understand the role place can play in fiction.

Gardner's exercise asks the writer to imagine a building— he doesn't specify what kind of building, so it could be a house, an office complex, a skyscraper, or a barn—and describe it "as seen by a man whose son has just been killed in a war." You can imagine how the man's sorrow might influence his view of the building. Gardner goes on, though, and instructs the writer to "not mention the son, war, death, or the old man doing the seeing."[6]

The brilliance of this exercise is how it reinforces the idea that setting—in this case the exterior of a man-made structure—is not static description, not an architect's rendering put into words, not divorced from character and your primal story, but intimately connected.

Gardner has a second half to this exercise as well, instructing the writer to describe "the same building, in the same weather and at the same time of day, as seen by a happy lover. Do not mention love or the loved one."

This challenge is every bit as applicable to memoir as it is to fiction, and entirely appropriate for a written description of the inside of a living room, a country kitchen, a field of corn, or an urban landscape of twisted fence and cracked concrete. The mental state of the narrator (a character or a memoir's author), the circumstances of the story (at the particular juncture where the description appears), and the heart story, or Invisible Magnetic River, of the book should be central to how the setting is described.

Or to put it another way, if you and I and forty other authors were writing forty-two different books, and each of us described what we, or our main character, saw from the deck of the Staten Island Ferry as it approached lower Manhattan in a winter snow squall, our descriptions should each be as different from one another as the individual snowflakes swirling in the frigid wind.

Now you try it. You can give Gardner's suggested circumstances a go, tackle one of the three variations that follow, or design your own based on the book you are writing now and the places you need to breathe life into:

1. Describe an elementary school playground as seen by a child walking toward his or her first day of school. Don't mention that it is the first day, or the child's particular fears or expectations. (Then, describe the same playground as the child leaves on the last day of school, anticipating a three-month summer break.)

2. Describe a physician's examination room as your main character is sitting alone, waiting for the oncologist to enter with news as to whether a small stomach tumor has been determined to be malignant or benign. Don't mention cancer, or tumor, or disease. (Then, describe the same examination room just after the doctor has left, leaving the patient behind to slowly gather her possessions. The patient has just been given a clean bill of health.)

3. Describe a sheep farm, with a small farmhouse and two outbuildings, on a hilly thirty acres or so, as your main character travels up the long driveway just twenty minutes after she signed the legal documents to own the property, a dream come true. Don't mention the mortgage, the real estate transaction, or the dream. Just describe what she sees. (Then, describe the same ride up the driveway as the narrator returns from the veterinarian with three sick lambs in the back of her pickup, dead-tired and discouraged by all that her lifelong fantasy entails.)

[

"I want to believe in something and what better than the world I can see, smell, touch, hear, and feel?"

—BARBARA HAMBY[1]

]

4 | THE LIFEBLOOD TEST

SCENE AND SENSORY DETAIL

If you are an avid reader, you already know that a well-written story brought vividly to life through exquisite detail, colorful language, active verbs, and vibrant nouns, amounts to so much more than just words on the page providing specific information. Novels and memoirs that captivate readers do so because they are an experience, an escape into a new world, a voyage of sorts, allowing us to feel how it might be to briefly live a life different than the one we've been given.

This experience goes back to the most primitive storytelling days, the gathering of our distant ancestors around a communal fire, the long-ago beginnings of our great myths and heroes' journeys. Over all of this time, the basics of what makes a story compelling have changed little.

Interestingly, though, over the last two decades or so scientists have been able to track this process of story engagement, using new technologies that allow us to map which parts of our brain "light up" as we engage in certain activities.

Benjamin K. Bergen, one of the cognitive scientists at the forefront of these recent findings on brain activity, tracked hand and eye movement, reaction times, and patterns revealed by magnetic resonance imaging (MRI) technology, to disprove previous assertions that language is processed only in certain centers in the brain—"Broca's area" and "Wernicke's area" to be exact. Instead, Bergen and others have determined that we process certain types of language in parts of the brain we previously thought were reserved for seeing and controlling movement.

So for instance, to use Bergen's own example, when a human subject encounters the sentence, "the shortstop threw the ball to first base," rather than simply registering the meaning of these words, separate parts of the subject's brain dedicated to vision and movement are activated.

Bergen explained his findings to National Public Radio in this way: "The way that you understand an action is by re-creating in your vision system what it would look like . . . and re-creating in your motor system what it would be like to be that shortstop, to have the ball in your hand and release it. . . . When you encounter words describing a particular action, your brain simulates the experience."[2]

Moreover, Canadian psychologists using similar brain-mapping technology have found that when reading stories, we also engage those specific neural networks that, in our everyday lives, we use to navigate encounters with other individuals—particularly encounters that require us to make sense of what others are thinking and feeling. The way we understand characters on the page, this research proved, closely mirrors the way we make sense of real folks who enter our lives.

Or in other words, well-crafted language creates a virtual reality, a manufactured experience strong enough to make us cringe, smile, blush, feel sadness, exult, and lose our breath. Stories fire those parts of our neural networks that help us to traverse real situations of curiosity, wonder, concern, and anxiety. People on the page can be as fascinating to us as their flesh-and-blood counterparts.

All of this from what are basically just abstract black marks lined up in rows on white paper.

Lighting Up the Reader

What this means is that writers need to be deliberate in filling each page with language that allows a reader to feel emotion, to experience a sense of movement, to join in with the characters' comfort or discomfort, the joy or sadness. We need to explicitly reward a reader's natural curiosity about the characters we create.

The language that will trigger a reader's neural synapses is sensory language: meaning simply, language that appeals to our senses.

Examine this sentence:

> I remember how wonderful Christmas morning used to be when the children were still young.

Or, in a novel:

> Carol remembered how wonderful Christmas morning used to be when the children were still young.

Nothing in either variation appeals to our sense of sight, smell, taste, touch, or hearing, short of the word Christmas, which might—just might, depending on the reader—evoke memories of pine sap, baked ham, colored lights, or figgy puddings. But even those sensory reactions are out of your control, part of the reader's story rather than the story you intend to be sharing.

Instead, we need sentences like these:

> The moments after Sarah and Tyler reached the bottom step and peered around the corner to see the presents piled under the brightly lit tree were always filled with giggles. In quick succession they would ask, "Now, Daddy? Now do we open them?" But Carol would still be in the kitchen preparing breakfast, filling the house with the aromas of toasted wheat bread, baked egg and cheese

casserole, and crisp sizzling bacon. "We have to wait for your mom," George would admonish the children, and they would pretend to be sad, lowering the corners of their mouths dramatically. If you looked closely, though, you could see enjoyment in their eyes and sense their rising delight as they ran hands over silky-smooth wrapping paper and lifted each box and wrapped present to gauge the weight, trying to guess at the contents. The sounds of pots and pans and metal utensils clanking in the kitchen had become so familiar over the years, it might well be the family Christmas carol. "Go in and help her, Daddy," Sarah would say. "The faster we eat, the sooner we see what Santa brought."

A mere point of fact—Christmas morning used to be "wonderful . . . when the children were still young"—is replaced by smells, color, texture and weight, movement, gasps of anticipation, and clanking pots and pans. The reader's brain is engaged fully, as if the reader were actually there, sitting front and center in the manufactured scene or reconstructed memory.

Joseph Conrad wrote his novel *Heart of Darkness* more than a century before cognitive scientists began using MRI studies to map readers' brains, but he knew the power of sensory detail all the same. He explained back then, "My task, which I am trying to achieve is, by the power of the written word, to make you hear, to make you feel—it is, above all, to make you see."[3]

Look at this excerpt from *Heart of Darkness*, as Marlow and his crew journey up the Congo River to find the mysterious Kurtz:

> The current was more rapid now, the steamer seemed at her last gasp, the stern-wheel flopped languidly, and I caught myself listening on tiptoe for the next beat of the boat, for in sober truth I expected the wretched thing to give up every moment. It was like watching the last flickers of a life.[4]

I would not advise you to mimic Conrad's syntax or diction—just a century or so later it seems outdated and stiff—but notice how he crafts his description so that we aren't just informed that the boat is old and likely to fail; instead, we, alongside the narrator, are "listening on tiptoe for the next beat" of the engine.

Here's more, from the same early passage:

> As we had plenty of wood, and caution was the word, I brought up in the middle of the stream. The reach was narrow, straight, with high sides like a railway cutting. The dusk came gliding into it long before the sun had set. The current ran smooth and swift, but a dumb immobility sat on the banks. The living trees, lashed together by the creepers and every living bush of the undergrowth, might have been changed into stone, even to the slenderest twig, to the lightest leaf. It was not sleep—it seemed unnatural, like a state of trance. Not the faintest sound of any kind could be heard. You looked on amazed, and began to suspect yourself of being deaf—then the night came suddenly, and struck you blind as well. About three in the morning some large fish leaped, and the loud splash made me jump as though a gun had been fired.[5]

Conrad's description of the physical world surrounding the aging sternwheeler as it idled mid-river is not only visually rich—"The living trees, lashed together by the creepers . . ."—but it invokes in us a sense of claustrophobia, allows us to feel how the jungle along the banks seemed to be closing in on Marlow and his crew, and how the stillness began quickly to seem sinister.

Finally, here is what follows, as morning comes and Conrad's narrator wakes to an unsettling surprise:

> When the sun rose there was a white fog, very warm and clammy, and more blinding than the night. It did not shift or drive; it was just there, standing all round you like

something solid. At eight or nine, perhaps, it lifted as a shutter lifts. We had a glimpse of the towering multitude of trees, of the immense matted jungle, with the blazing little ball of the sun hanging over it—all perfectly still—and then the white shutter came down again, smoothly, as if sliding in greased grooves. I ordered the chain, which we had begun to heave in, to be paid out again. Before it stopped running with a muffled rattle, a cry, a very loud cry, as of infinite desolation, soared slowly in the opaque air. It ceased. A complaining clamor, modulated in savage discords, filled our ears. The sheer unexpectedness of it made my hair stir under my cap. I don't know how it struck the others: to me it seemed as though the mist itself had screamed, so suddenly, and apparently from all sides at once, did this tumultuous and mournful uproar arise.[6]

The fog is not just heavy, it is "warm and clammy . . . blinding . . ." and stood "all round you like something solid." Along with this suffocating damp blanket, we experience not just an unexpected sound, a shrill sound, or a painful cry, but a "complaining clamor, modulated in savage discords . . . as though the mist itself had screamed, so suddenly, and apparently from all sides at once . . ."[7]

Conrad's sensory detail is filtered through the vulnerability of the moment, and tied directly to the protagonists' point of view, attaching his fears and premonitions to every inch of jungle greenery and each ripple on the river's surface.

His details are also magnetically pulled toward the heart story—dare I say Invisible Magnetic Congo River?—with *all* of our senses aroused (and multiple pathways of our neural network brightly flashing).

The Undeniable Importance of Scene

When you add together complex characterization, dialogue that resembles actual human conversation rather than exposition or explanation, a tactile feel of setting and place, and rich sensory detail, what you have is scene.

Scene is what people mean when they say "show, don't tell."

Scene is what you see each time you watch a movie: specific human beings, in a particular place, surrounded by particular objects, moving through time. Usually, though not always, the human beings are interacting in some way. Most likely they are talking.

Scene is the blood that fills the body of story. Without it, the patient dies.

Remember, though, that a scene is more than a photograph.

This, for instance, is not a scene, despite the quantity of description:

> My grandmother's house was filled top to bottom with little statues and figurines of the angels she had collected for most of her seventy years. She had a dining room table that stretched from one end of the large room to the other end, with enough chairs to fit the entire family for holiday celebrations, jolly times when she would often make ham, scalloped potatoes, and endless side dishes, or perhaps roast a turkey with two kinds of dressing. She kept three crystal decanters on an oak sideboard that had once belonged to her Italian immigrant mother; one decanter held red wine, another held amber-colored whiskey, and the third was filled with an odd green liqueur, one that smelled like mint and tasted like cough syrup.

This, on the other hand, is a scene:

> I stepped into my grandmother's living room, only to find Uncle Tony splayed out on his back, snoring on the maroon wool carpet. He had clearly been hitting with unusual eagerness one of the crystal decanters where Grandmom Maria stored the liquor. Usually, he didn't pass out until *after* dinner.
>
> My niece Delia had taken six of Grandmom's angel figurines from atop the piano and was placing them in various spots along Uncle Tony's chest. "He's dead," she told me in her endearing three-year-old voice. "The angels will help him find his way to heaven."
>
> Most of my cousins were in the adjoining dining room, seated at the table where Grandmom had already begun to place side dishes of green beans, mashed potatoes, sweet potato casserole, sweet corn, and a Jell-O salad with green grapes. The table barely had room for plates and silverware.
>
> "Lisa," my cousin Bill shouted. "Why so late? We thought you had defected to North Korea."
>
> Bill's wife Sally groaned and patted a chair for me. "Sit here."
>
> "Who's that?" Grandmom called out from the open kitchen doorway. "Who just came in? Do we have enough chairs?"
>
> "Yes Grandmom," Bill hollered back. "It's the prodigal Lisa."
>
> "Well make her comfortable, and would someone please hide the whiskey, then wake up poor Tony? The ham is coming out in three minutes."

Scene is where your readers can lose themselves, forget they are even reading a book, and just drink in the action. (That pun may or may not have been intended.)

Here is an example from the classic *Treasure Island*, by Robert Louis Stevenson. Notice how Stevenson lets the scene spin out in real time, allowing readers to experience for themselves the initial curiosity, then fascination, and finally, the slight discomfort felt by the young narrator, Jim Hawkins:

It was one January morning, very early—a pinching, frosty morning—the cove all grey with hoar-frost, the ripple lapping softly on the stones, the sun still low and only touching the hilltops and shining far to seaward. The captain had risen earlier than usual and set out down the beach, his cutlass swinging under the broad skirts of the old blue coat, his brass telescope under his arm, his hat tilted back upon his head. . . .

Well, mother was upstairs with father and I was laying the breakfast-table against the captain's return when the parlour door opened and a man stepped in on whom I had never set my eyes before. He was a pale, tallowy creature, wanting two fingers of the left hand, and though he wore a cutlass, he did not look much like a fighter. I had always my eye open for seafaring men, with one leg or two, and I remember this one puzzled me. He was not sailorly, and yet he had a smack of the sea about him too.

I asked him what was for his service, and he said he would take rum; but as I was going out of the room to fetch it, he sat down upon a table and motioned me to draw near. I paused where I was, with my napkin in my hand.

"Come here, sonny," says he. "Come nearer here."

I took a step nearer.

"Is this here table for my mate Bill?" he asked with a kind of leer.

I told him I did not know his mate Bill, and this was for a person who stayed in our house whom we called the captain.

"Well," said he, "my mate Bill would be called the captain, as like as not. He has a cut on one cheek and a mighty pleasant way with him, particularly in drink, has my mate Bill. We'll put it, for argument like, that your captain has a cut on one cheek—and we'll put it, if you like, that that cheek's the right one. Ah, well! I told you. Now, is my mate Bill in this here house?"

I told him he was out walking.

"Which way, sonny? Which way is he gone?"[8]

Recall those Canadian psychologists who determined that well-told stories trigger the precise parts of our brain that fire up when we are attempting to make sense of the real people in our daily lives. Stevenson's brief scene with the stranger allows us to puzzle out this odd visitor right alongside the young boy, and that sort of active engagement is precisely what keeps us reading.

By the way, readers have a responsibility in this process as well, their own role in releasing the power of sensory detail and carefully crafted scene. Listen to novelist Francine Prose speaking directly to readers, explaining the flip side of the equation:

> With so much reading ahead of you, the temptation might be to speed up. But in fact it's essential to slow down and read every word. Because one important thing that can be learned by reading slowly is the seemingly obvious but oddly underappreciated fact that language is the medium we use in much the same way a composer uses notes, the way a painter uses paint. I realize it may seem obvious, but it's surprising how easily we lose sight of the fact that words are the raw material out of which literature is crafted.[9]

Reward your readers with prose that stands up to slowing down and reading every word.

If you think of the words in your novel or memoir not as mere carriers of meaning, but as oil paint layered onto the canvas, the raw material of an unseen world you are trying to bring to life, you're on the right track.

🧰 THE BOOK DOCTOR MAKES A HOUSE CALL

The Cure for Common Problems with Scene and Sensory Detail

One important step in adding sensory detail to your writing is to begin noticing it more deliberately in the actual world. Human beings see, hear, smell, taste, and touch on a regular basis, but sometimes we don't take the time to register these sensory experiences. The diagnoses, cures, exercises, and prompts in this section will help alleviate that symptom.

❶ DIAGNOSIS: You Only Have Two Senses to Rub Together

Quite frequently beginning writers—or for that matter, experienced writers working through a first or second draft—will construct scenes that rely almost entirely on two senses: sight and sound. Visual details are often the first to come to mind, and auditory details are often provided through dialogue, essentially the words spoken and perhaps some sense of how the words are conveyed.

Both of those are well and good, but just a fraction of what is possible, and of what is needed to make a scene complete.

➡ THE CURE

There is so much we overlook. Suppose our two main characters, in novel or memoir, are standing in the living room having a conversation. Well, this conversation takes place in a world of sensory input.

Consider other sounds beyond the words these two characters share. Is there a radio (or Pandora station on someone's laptop) playing in the kitchen? Are there traffic noises coming in through an open window? Is the neighbor's dog barking? How about the distant whine of a chainsaw coming from a quarter mile away?

I grew up in a small, industrial Pennsylvania city, on 9th Street, a quiet block of modest, two-story houses. Twelfth Street, however, was just three blocks south of us, and that wide thoroughfare was where—because of where the railroad lines were situated—heavy industry had built up over the years. The entirety of my childhood played out against a backdrop of train whistles and iron forges, distant booming noises that were barely perceptible but present nonetheless during the months our windows were closed, and impossible to ignore on still summer evenings when windows were left wide open to the breeze.

Most places are like this. Isolated farms have cows, sheep, dogs, or chickens, along with tractors, threshers, and other farming equipment, all adding ambient sound to whatever is occurring in the kitchen or on the porch. Urban locations have honking taxis, blaring sirens, delivery trucks, and construction noise. Even quiet suburbs have car doors slamming, children laughing in the neighbor's backyard, squawking crows or singing sparrows.

What are you leaving out?

And that is just our sense of hearing.

Our sense of smell also comes into play constantly, even if we aren't paying close attention: consider the perfume, cologne, or shampoo of someone just momentarily passing by, the smell of fried food coming out of an apartment window or restaurant vent, dumpsters, truck exhaust, cigarette smoke.

Our sense of touch is active too. The book you are holding, the lip balm, the glass of iced tea, all have a particular feel. We brush up against doorways, cinder-block walls, prickly bushes, most any time we take a walk. We reach down to touch our own clothing, or we reach into our pockets and feel keys, coins, bills, a handkerchief, or balls of lint. If your novel or memoir features the point of view of a child, consider how often at that age you picked up sticks to inspect them, turned rocks over in your palm, cracked open acorns with your fingernail, or pulled dandelions. At my current age, I am constantly stroking my chin and being surprised at how fast my whiskers return.

Finally, there is taste.

If your characters are having lunch in a cozy bistro, munching crisp salad and sipping seafood bisque, bringing the sense of taste onto the page may come easily enough, but even in scenes that are not restaurant-centric, remember that we also chew gum, suck lozenges, obsessively pop breath mints; that the taste of breakfast can linger in our mouths for hours; that medicines we take can leave an aftertaste, as does toothpaste; and that even the air we breathe can have its own flavor, depending on whether we are near a chemical plant, the seashore, or a wheat field on a windy day.

❷ DIAGNOSIS: When You're Writing, It All Comes Out as Summary

It makes sense that our first attempt to create a moment between two characters in a novel, or re-create a remembered moment in our memoir, will end up on the page as more summary than fully developed scene. We imagine these moments (or remember them) in fits and starts, sketching out the surface action first, and hopefully filling in other details later. The normal human urge to rush on to the next page and next moment, though, might occasionally tempt us to leave these scenes half-done.

▤▷ THE CURE

Here is one of those "just take your medicine whether you like it or not" prescriptions: scenes are necessary, integral, indispensable to good storytelling, but they are also *much more difficult to write than mere summary.*

They take more time.

They take more concentration.

They take more imagination (or memory recall).

At my writing desk, a summary paragraph that serves as a placeholder for a full scene I intend to write later might mean ten to fifteen minutes at the keyboard. Writing the scene itself, which includes visualizing it moment to moment so the puzzle pieces fit together neatly, then checking and rechecking that the details are vibrant and correct, and scrutinizing even further to ensure that every moment aligns with the characters and situation being described, could take me a full day at the keyboard for a scene that stretches out to three or four pages.

Scenes are what allow the readers to feel as if they are exactly there, living the moment alongside the characters. Tough, necessary, and rewarding work.

PROMPTS AND EXERCISES TO CURE SCENE AND SENSORY DETAIL PROBLEMS

Whether you are writing about yourself in memoir or inventing characters for a novel, remember that human beings live in a physical world, filled with physical sensations. The more you can bring that world to life in your writing, the better your book will be.

IS YOUR WRITING OUT OF TOUCH?

Fine, that happens, but perhaps what you need to do is immediately step away from the keyboard and go touch some things. I mean this literally. Remind yourself of the tactile world you inhabit.

Here are some words to describe how things feel on our fingers, on our cheeks, or on our arms or legs as we brush up against them:

- Abrasive

- Bristly

- Cool

- Cushioned

- Firm

- Knobbed

- Mushy

- Pliable

- Sharp-edged

- Sticky

- Velvety

Can you add ten more?

_____

_____

_____

_____

_____

_____

_____

_____

_____

_____

Now, with all of this fresh in your mind, get back to writing that scene. (But don't overdo. The goal is not to layer in every word possible, or to overwhelm the reader. The goal is to get the *right* detail, in the *right* place.)

THING ONE AND THING TWO

One additional reason that scenes on the page often fail to resemble real life is the tendency to have our characters focus on one thing at a time, whereas out here in the real world, the "not on the page" world, we are almost always focusing on more than one—often, three to five—different goals or activities.

Consider the last time you argued with a spouse or romantic partner. Did you stand at attention and argue your points systematically, or was one of you chopping up carrots and tomatoes for the dinner salad while the other one ripped open that day's mail and sorted it into bills, flyers, and junk?

Or think about your most recent visit to your parents' home. As you strolled in the front door, did Mom and Dad drop everything and simply give you their complete attention, or did your father welcome you while continuing to fiddle with the TV remote, at the same time that your mother shouted "Oh, how nice of you to drop by without calling first" while scurrying around the room to clean up what she called "such a total mess"?

If you have children, and you knock on the bedroom door to discuss plans for the weekend, do the kids stop playing their video games right in the middle of the action because what you have to say is so important? (If your answer is "yes," you should consider writing a book titled *Miracle Parenting*.)

Assemble for yourself a list of things we do while doing other things:

- Do you talk on the phone while unpacking groceries in your kitchen and lifting the cans and boxes onto the shelves and into the cabinets?

- Are you unloading the dishwasher at the same time that you supervise your daughter's after-school homework?

- What do you do while waiting at a stoplight?

- What else are you doing while sitting at your desk at work answering emails?

- In the act of emptying the dryer and folding the clothes, are you more like a Buddhist monk or a whirling dervish?

If you are writing a novel, look back at your scenes and consider whether you've missed the opportunity to give your characters authenticity by allowing them to be distracted, to multitask, to lurch and shuffle through the day like real, overburdened souls.

If you are writing a memoir, remember these scenes from your past as vividly as possible, but remember as well what *else* was going on.

"An appealing voice achieves an intimate connection—a bond much stronger than the kind forged, intellectually, through crafted writing."

—STEPHEN KING[1]

5 | A VISIT WITH THE THROAT AND EYE DOCTORS

VOICE AND POINT OF VIEW

In the preceding chapters, we've looked at prose elements vital to the heart story itself and those essential to fully establishing perceptible, believable characters moving through an observable, credible world. Of equal importance are two key elements of the writing craft that revolve around *who* is telling the story and from *what angle* the story is being told.

Voice is the first thing your reader encounters, starting on page one, with the very first word. As we'll discuss, the predominant voice, the one telling the story, is in almost all cases either the voice of the character who narrates or the voice of the author herself, but beyond that, countless permutations are possible.

Point of view begins immediately as well, and goes beyond the simple mechanics of first-, second-, or third-person narration. From what angle are the events on the page being seen? Through whose sensibility, understanding, and biases is the story being passed along?

So, if you would, please cough for the Book Doctor and blink a few times.

Let's have a look at the health of your book's throat and eyes.

Notes from the Throat Doctor: Clarity of Voice

The array of voices possible in your novel or memoir is limitless, with only two irrefutable rules.

1. Don't ignore voice.

2. Establish a clear voice that makes the reader want to stay around.

I'll assume you aren't going to violate the first rule, since you are already this far into the chapter. The second rule can be trickier, perhaps, but as you've probably realized by now, the phrase "this sure does get tricky" is so true that it ought to be tattooed on every writer's forearm.

If you are attempting to write a book, every bit of the challenge becomes tricky, like juggling eight tennis balls at the same time, while riding a unicycle. That's why writing a book can be so exciting. And so damn hard.

So what is voice? On the page, in your book, voice is some combination of your prose style (the words you choose, the length and pattern of your sentences, the rhythm and music you create with language) and the storyteller's personality.

Let's look at style first.

Prose style can be something subtle or very pronounced. Ernest Hemingway, for instance, created a style that many find instantly recognizable.

Read this, from the opening of *A Farewell to Arms:*

> In the late summer of that year we lived in a house in a village that looked across the river and the plain to the mountains. In the bed of the river there were pebbles and boulders, dry and white in the sun, and the water was clear and swiftly moving and blue in the channels. Troops went by the house and down the road and the dust they raised powdered the leaves of the trees. The trunks of the trees too were dusty and the leaves fell early that year and we saw the troops marching along the road and the dust rising and leaves, stirred by the breeze, falling and the

soldiers marching and afterward the road bare and white except for the leaves.[2]

Hemingway is often remembered for his short, unadorned sentences, and certainly some of his work demonstrates those traits, but notice as well the number of one- or two-syllable words used in the description—dry, white, clear, dusty, bare. That too is a Hemingway trademark: not because he lacked the vocabulary, but because he favored the effect.

The final sentence in the paragraph is, in fact, a bit on the longer side for Mr. Hemingway: fifty words. But he had good reason. The rhythm and repetition are likely meant to evoke a sense of marching in a reader's mind; not necessarily in a way that a reader would even notice, but there nonetheless.

Joan Didion is another writer whose style identifies her work almost immediately. Here is a snippet from the opening chapter of the memoir she wrote the year after her husband died, *The Year of Magical Thinking*:

> Life changes in the instant.
> The ordinary instant.
> At some point, in the interest of remembering what seemed most striking about what had happened, I considered adding those words, "the ordinary instant." I saw immediately that there would be no need to add the word "ordinary," because there would be no forgetting it: the word never left my mind. It was in fact the ordinary nature of everything preceding the event that prevented me from truly believing it had happened, absorbing it, incorporating it, getting past it. I recognize now that there was nothing unusual in this: confronted with sudden disaster we all focus on how unremarkable the circumstances were in which the unthinkable occurred, the clear blue sky from which the plane fell, the routine

errand that ended on the shoulder with the car in flames, the swings where the children were playing as usual when the rattlesnake struck from the ivy.[3]

Didion's style, unlike Hemingway's, has less to do with word choice and more to do with how she so often dissects the words she is writing, even as she writes them, and how her sentences reflect her thinking, and her tendency to double back and reexamine. Like the work of the earliest essayists, the European forerunners of the modern memoir form, the movement of this passage reflects not a character's movement across the room but the movement of Didion's inquisitive mind.

Which brings us to personality.

In memoir, the personality front and center on the page is that of the author, who is also the main character, and the narrator. Think of Elizabeth Gilbert's opening line, "I wish Giovanni would kiss me." You can't get much more personal than that.

Or this from the opening page of James Baldwin's *Notes of a Native Son*:

> In those days my mother was given to the exasperating and mysterious habit of having babies. As they were born, I took them over with one hand and held a book with the other. The children probably suffered, though they have since been kind enough to deny it, and in this way I read *Uncle Tom's Cabin* and *A Tale of Two Cities* over and over again; in this way, in fact, I read just about everything I could get my hands on—except the Bible, probably because it was the only book I was encouraged to read.[4]

Baldwin's wit, intellect, and contrary nature are all on display, in words that could hardly be more simple or direct.

Or have a look at the opening of Dorothy Allison's *Two or Three Things I Know for Sure*:

> "Let me tell you a story," I used to whisper to my sisters, hiding with them behind the red-dirt bean hills and row on row of strawberries. My sisters' faces were thin and sharp, with high cheekbones and restless eyes, like my mama's face, my Aunt Dot's, my own. Peasants, that's what we are and always have been.[5]

Allison is not just relaying information; she is offering attitude.

In a novel, the personality that peeks hesitantly (or shines brightly) through each sentence may be that of a main character, may be that of an invented narrator, or in some cases may shift between characters. As in memoir, the voice and personality of a novel's narrator might reflect geography, education, rural simplicity versus urban sophistication, ethnic background, social class, or any number of other factors.

Take for instance the opening passage from *The Adventures of Huckleberry Finn*, by Mark Twain:

> You don't know about me without you have read a book by the name of *The Adventures of Tom Sawyer*; but that ain't no matter. That book was made by Mr. Mark Twain, and he told the truth, mainly. There was things which he stretched, but mainly he told the truth. That is nothing. I never seen anybody but lied one time or another, without it was Aunt Polly, or the widow, or maybe Mary. Aunt Polly—Tom's Aunt Polly, she is—and Mary, and the Widow Douglas is all told about in that book, which is mostly a true book, with some stretchers, as I said before.

Now the way that the book winds up is this:

> Tom and me found the money that the robbers hid in the cave, and it made us rich. We got six thousand dollars

apiece—all gold. It was an awful sight of money when it was piled up. Well, Judge Thatcher he took it and put it out at interest, and it fetched us a dollar a day apiece all the year round—more than a body could tell what to do with. The Widow Douglas she took me for her son, and allowed she would sivilize me; but it was rough living in the house all the time, considering how dismal regular and decent the widow was in all her ways; and so when I couldn't stand it no longer I lit out. I got into my old rags and my sugar-hogshead again, and was free and satisfied. But Tom Sawyer he hunted me up and said he was going to start a band of robbers, and I might join if I would go back to the widow and be respectable. So I went back.[6]

You might take notice immediately of the grammatical inconsistencies and regional idiosyncrasies, but there is also a distinctly irreverent tone and straight-faced humor. Most readers will smile broadly at the notion that Huck must first go back to Widow Douglas and become respectable again before he can join Tom Sawyer's band of crooks.

Another excellent example is a paragraph from the opening chapter of Lee Martin's novel *The Bright Forever*, a 2006 finalist for the Pulitzer Prize for Fiction:

I've never been able to tell this story and my part in it until now, but listen, I'll say it true: a man can live with something like this only so long before he has to make it known. My name is Henry Dees, and I was a teacher then—a teacher of mathematics and a summer tutor for the children like Katie who needed such a thing. I'm an old man now, and even though more than thirty years have gone by, I still remember that summer and its secrets, and the way the heat was and how the light stretched on into evening like it would never leave. If you want to listen, you'll have to trust me. Or close the book;

go back to your lives. I warn you: this is a story as hard to hear as it is for me to tell.[7]

The phrase "I'll say it true" rings out like a bell in that passage, as does the quiet admonition, "If you want to listen, you'll have to trust me. Or close the book; go back to your lives." The setting is important as well: the way that Henry Dees describes the summer light seems to suggest something about the tragic secrets he is about to share.

HOW DO WE FIND OUR VOICE?

Lee Martin, author of the preceding passage, was born in southeastern Illinois, where his father farmed eighty acres in Lawrence County. It is a very rustic part of Illinois, flat and harsh, but like most places, beautiful in its own way. Lee and I are friends, and I know how important his rural roots are to how he writes.

Here he is in an interview, discussing how his birthplace influenced the subject matter and texture of his novels and memoirs:

> As the son of a farmer, I grew up very aware of the way the seasons and changes in weather affected our livelihood. This connection between the individual and the natural world became elemental to me, something that couldn't be broken. I learned as I aged that I was who I was in part because of where I was.[8]

On his blog, Lee expands on this idea, and talks about how he drew inspiration from Richard Ford's writing, particularly the way Ford brought the voices of his native Montana neighbors to life in his story collection *Rock Springs*.

> Beginning writers, when it comes to choosing their material, often overlook that which is nearest to them.

They cast their eyes elsewhere because they assume no one will be interested in the subject matter that they know the best and that's the most significant for them. I fell into that trap myself. I thought stories about my small town and farming community weren't worth writing about because sophisticated readers would never be interested. Then I heard the voice of Richard Ford, in his collection *Rock Springs*, and even though he was writing mostly about the American West, I heard something in his direct and understated approach that was familiar. That was the way the men from my native southeastern Illinois spoke: restrained, but with a bit of an edge, as they went directly about the business of telling the stories they had to tell.[9]

The list of outstanding writers for whom both their written voice and the voices of their primary characters stemmed from the regions and communities where they spent their early lives is a very long list indeed. Think William Faulkner, Flannery O'Connor, Frank McCourt, or Maya Angelou. Think Larry McMurtry. Amy Tan. Richard Rodriguez. Garrison Keillor. Mark Twain.

It is not a requirement that we write novels set in the rural (or urban, or suburban) landscape of our youth, of course, or for that matter, that we set our novels in the country where we live. Imagination and the willingness to do the necessary research allow authors all of the latitude they choose. (In science fiction, you needn't even stay on your home planet.)

Still, the shortest path to an authentic voice is to look inside and listen for the words and phrasings that come naturally, that reflect who you are as a person.

While our voice on the page can be very close to our informal speech, voice in writing is not *exactly* like speech. Our actual way of speaking goes beyond just words, to include tone of voice, facial expressions (winks, nods, smiles), and physical signals (shrugs, hand gestures).

Author and critic Louis Menand points out as well that speech is spontaneous, whereas writing is not, at least not when it has been revised:

> Some writers write many drafts of a piece; some write one draft, at the pace of a snail after a night on the town. But chattiness, slanginess, in-your-face-ness, and any other features of writing that are conventionally characterized as "like speech" are usually the results of laborious experimentation, revision, calibration, walks around the block, unnecessary phone calls, and recalibration. . . . Writers are not mere copyists of language; they are polishers, embellishers, perfecters. They spend hours getting the timing right—so that what they write sounds completely unrehearsed.[10]

So it is good to aim for writing that is "like" natural speech, but polished and processed.

Note Menand's mention of a final product that "sounds completely unrehearsed." When we read an author whose voice seems so "natural," the normal tendency is to imagine it came easily to the writer, but this is mostly illusion: great prose is more often than not the result of diligent revision and long labor.

Too often, though, even before we have the chance to revise and polish, we strangle our own voices, squeezing out precisely those elements that readers want to hear. This is a beginner's mistake for the most part, some misguided notion of erudition that we seem to acquire in grade school or high school, this sense that adding unnecessary formality to our voices will make us seem smarter or more significant.

It doesn't.

As a college teacher, I read a fair number of dull essays and lifeless short stories every semester. They seem to be written by machine, not reflective of someone with a heart and a soul or any intrinsic individuality. I'll often find myself sitting woefully at my desk, shaking my head back and forth, underlining sentences that go on forever yet say nothing, and circling multisyllabic words that sound impressive but are used imprecisely, or at times, it seems, just randomly.

And then I'll get up from my desk, walk out into the hallway of my classroom building, and overhear these very same students telling one another stories about silly things that happened over the past weekend, or about dramatic events in their personal lives. They suddenly sound committed, passionate, and full of life. The expressions they use make me giggle inside. And I think, "*Damn*, if they could just get some of that energy onto the page . . . if they showed half that enthusiasm . . . then we'd have something."

Just as children seem to lose their sense of playfulness and creativity as they grow into adulthood, writers too often seem to lose touch with what makes their own voice and viewpoint colorful, textured, surprising, and unique.

Well, cripes yiminy, y'all: *Don't do that.*

TAKE A HEARING TEST

Here's another secret:

Many writers actually write and revise out loud.

I certainly do. If you were sitting outside my office door when I was shoulder-deep in a complex writing project, you would hear me talking to myself, literally. (I sometimes imagine someone on the other side of the door thinking, "Oh my goodness, Dinty's losing his mind.") But I'm not speaking to invisible demons, I'm auditioning various ways of phrasing an idea or moment, reciting two or three slightly altered sentence forms to see which one hits the right note, and working on rhythm. Once I like the way a sentence or passage sounds, I'll move on to step two, asking myself, "Does that sentence that now sounds the way I want it to sound actually say something?"

I often trust my ear more than my brain. Words are complicated, slippery little critters, but my ear can usually sense when something is slightly (or horribly) off.

Once my sentences sound right, and when it also sounds to me as if the sentences carry meaning, by offering an appropriate image or sensory detail, by providing precise information without excess baggage, by living and breathing on the page, then I've found my authentic voice.

Notes from the Eye Doctor: Focusing on Point of View

In the best writing, voice and point of view join together in a single strand, reinforcing one another, creating a unified whole. I'll talk about the way these two craft elements connect to become a sum greater than its parts in a moment, but first let's get the basics out of the way.

In a strictly mechanical sense, point of view in storytelling simply delineates the differences between first-, second-, and third-person narration.

For instance:

> "I walked up to the editor who sent me the nasty rejection and punched him in the nose." (First person)
> "You walked up to the editor who sent you the nasty rejection and punched him in the nose." (Second person)
> "Nora the Novelist walked up to the editor who sent her the nasty rejection and punched him in the nose." (Third person)

The poor editor, but he probably deserved it.

Second, point of view in prose writing ties to whether your narrator's understanding of events is limited or omniscient.

Limited point of view means that what is seen, what is relayed, what is understood, what is sensed, what is dreamed, all comes from one person, the narrator or main character. (Some novels will switch narrators from chapter to chapter, and thus point of view shifts as well, but the limitations still apply within the chapter.)

So for instance, if you are writing in limited point of view, and your character punches her editor in the nose, and the editor then jumps into a taxi and speeds away, you (or your character) can tell readers what the editor looked like getting into the taxi, what vulgar curses he shouted out the window, and what the back of his head looked like as the taxi raced off, and not much more. Certainly not what the editor barked at his assistant when he returned to the office, or what revenge he is plotting.

Think of it this way: In real life, had you punched the editor who stupidly rejected your work, you wouldn't know what happened after the taxi sped off, and you wouldn't be able to read the editor's mind, so in limited point of view your narrator cannot either.

In real life, you might also end up facing assault charges, so be careful.

Omniscient, on the other hand, means "all knowing," the godlike ability to see and know everything going on in the world, even if the action is happening across town from where a central character is standing. We might see Nora the Novelist punch the editor in the schnozz, access her inner thoughts as she does so ("Take that, you illiterate weasel"), stay with her as she massages her sore knuckles, and remain at her side as she watches the taxi speed off. Then—usually after a line of white space—we as readers can show up in the corporate offices of Blind, Stupid & Crazy Publishing House to witness the editor kicking his wastebasket and screaming into the phone because his nose is broken and he can't reach his doctor.

All aspects of the story, the innermost thoughts of any and all characters, and all locations are open to us, if the writer chooses to take us there.

Memoir, by definition, is told in the first person, and the point of view is limited.

You, the author and main character, can speculate as to what your ex-husband was thinking when he ran off with the twenty-three-year-old dental assistant, and (if you must) you can imagine them lounging on a hotel bed, sipping mimosas, giving one another foot massages, pledging eternal love, but if you aren't there, you can't know.

A few authors have experimented with second- and third-person narration in memoir—as in all artistic arenas, writers like to bend and stretch conventions to see what new forms they can create—but these experiments are rare.

Probably someone has experimented with omniscient memoir as well, but unless the author is Santa Claus ("he sees you when you're sleeping, he knows when you're awake"), I'm not sure how that would work.

In the novel, anything goes, as long as you've made a conscious decision and remain consistent.

But the real power of point of view goes deeper, and is often linked directly to character. This is the unified whole, the sum greater than its parts, where point of view merges with voice.

In limited point of view, it is not just that the reader has access to only what the narrator or main characters see or hear—as if there is just one camera available in the world, and that camera is strapped to the narrator's forehead. Point of view also relates to viewpoint: *how* the person perceives the world.

The simplest way to illustrate my point is to imagine a child narrator. Little Maureen—let's say she is five or six—sees the same action and hears the same words that an adult in the room might see or hear, but she interprets the actions differently, often incorrectly—("I peeked through the doorway and Mommy and Daddy were in the bed, naked, and they were wrestling")—and she often can't comprehend the meaning behind certain words and phrases—("Mommy and Daddy were naked in the bed wrestling, but Mommy was praying, calling out to Jesus over and over").

A less slapstick illustration might be how someone who has been around horses her entire life experiences that moment just before the start of the Kentucky Derby when the competitors are being led to the gate—she notices things we might not notice, she interprets with greater clarity and depth. Yet another example would be how a victim of spousal abuse reacts when an angry man storms into a restaurant, shouting and waving his arms for no obvious reason. That same moment might be seen quite differently through the point of view of an off-duty police officer. A trained psychotherapist might have yet another reaction—she would notice different details, would likely emphasize different aspects of the story when she retells it later to her husband.

I'm an optimist and tend to see the world differently than how my more apprehensive friends see it. If you saw the world through my eyes, heard my thoughts as life unfolds before me, it would look and sound differently than if you saw all of this through the eyes of someone with deep pessimism or suspicion.

And the poor punching bag of an editor?

The moment when you sock him in the nose and he retreats to a taxi cab would undoubtedly look, feel, and sound quite different from his perspective. And to be honest, the story behind why your manuscript was rejected would look significantly different from his point of view as well. Maybe the publishing house is in dire financial straits. Maybe he loved your novel, but just weeks before it landed on his desk the publishing house he works for signed a contract for a book that was very similar. Maybe he was reading your memoir about the death of your beloved mother just weeks after he buried his own mom, and he just couldn't, on that particular day, muster up the distance or enthusiasm for a story that hit so close to home.

What we see through our two eyes isn't necessarily so different, but our viewpoint, our comprehension, our biases, our initial assessments, the hidden information at our disposal, and all the rest, are as varied as the tones of purple in the bruising along that poor punch-drunk editor's ravaged nose.

To illustrate point of view fully in action, look at how much we learn of Pip's personality and attitude toward the world around him, not just his observational skills, in this passage from Dickens's *Great Expectations*:

> My sister, Mrs. Joe Gargery, was more than twenty years older than I, and had established a great reputation with herself and the neighbors because she had brought me up "by hand." Having at that time to find out for myself what the expression meant, and knowing her to have a hard and heavy hand, and to be much in the habit of laying it upon her husband as well as upon me, I supposed that Joe Gargery and I were both brought up by hand.
>
> She was not a good-looking woman, my sister; and I had a general impression that she must have made Joe Gargery marry her by hand. Joe was a fair man, with curls of flaxen hair on each side of his smooth face, and with eyes of such a very undecided blue that they seemed to have somehow got mixed with their own whites. He was a mild, good-natured, sweet-tempered, easy-going, foolish, dear fellow—a sort of Hercules in strength, and also in weakness.
>
> My sister, Mrs. Joe, with black hair and eyes, had such a prevailing redness of skin that I sometimes used to wonder whether it was possible she washed herself with a nutmeg-grater instead of soap . . . [11]

In his novel *The Curious Incident of the Dog in the Night-Time*, Mark Haddon attempted an even more complicated rendering of point of view. His fictional narrator Christopher is not just a fifteen-year-old boy, seeing and understanding the world as a fifteen-year-old boy might, but he is also autistic. Specifically, he has a sort of high-functioning autism known as Asperger's syndrome, marked often by verbal peculiarities and a precise, literal viewpoint.

Here is the opening of that novel:

> It was 7 minutes after midnight. The dog was lying on the grass in the middle of the lawn in front of Mrs. Shears' house. Its eyes were closed. It looked as if it was running on its side, the way dogs run when they think they are chasing a cat in a dream. But the dog was not running or asleep. The dog was dead. There was a garden fork sticking out of the dog. The points of the fork must have gone all the way through the dog and into the ground because the fork had not fallen over. I decided that the dog was probably killed with the fork because I could not see any other wounds in the dog and I do not think you would stick a garden fork into a dog after it had died for some other reason, like cancer for example, or a road accident. But I could not be certain about this.[12]

Even third-person narration can be imbued with the main character's point of view. Consider how much of poor Dorothy's boredom and loneliness we sense in this excerpt from the opening pages of L. Frank Baum's *The Wonderful Wizard of Oz*:

> When Dorothy stood in the doorway and looked around, she could see nothing but the great gray prairie on every side. Not a tree nor a house broke the broad sweep of flat country that reached to the edge of the sky in all directions. The sun had baked the plowed land into a gray mass, with

little cracks running through it. Even the grass was not green, for the sun had burned the tops of the long blades until they were the same gray color to be seen everywhere. Once the house had been painted, but the sun blistered the paint and the rains washed it away, and now the house was as dull and gray as everything else.

When Aunt Em came there to live she was a young, pretty wife. The sun and wind had changed her, too. They had taken the sparkle from her eyes and left them a sober gray; they had taken the red from her cheeks and lips, and they were gray also. She was thin and gaunt, and never smiled now. . . .

Uncle Henry never laughed. He worked hard from morning till night and did not know what joy was. He was gray also, from his long beard to his rough boots, and he looked stern and solemn, and rarely spoke.

It was Toto that made Dorothy laugh, and saved her from growing as gray as her other surroundings . . . [13]

And finally, an example from the realm of memoir, from Brian Doyle's tiny gem of a book, *The Wet Engine: Exploring the Mad Wild Miracle of the Heart*:

Doctor Dave McIrvin is slight and thin and intense and smiling and one of those puzzling human creatures who while they are talking to you seem to have all the time in the universe, and look you right in the eye, and answer your questions directly and straightforwardly, and listen to what you say, and don't listen impatiently waiting for you to finish what foolish thing *you* are saying so *they* can tell you what wise thing they know, but as soon as you finish talking to Dave he is gone like a cat. He just is *gone*. It is the most amazing thing you ever saw. Because he is a doctor he almost always is wearing green scrubs so if you pay attention and watch carefully when he begins to be gone you will see a greenish whir and blur in the air topped by Dave's grin, and then the vision and Dave are both gone, and you are standing there thinking that old Lewis Carroll knew what he was talking about when he invented the Cheshire Cat.[14]

Doyle's memoir focuses on the heart defect that endangered the life of one of his infant twin sons, but the tone here is not sorrowful, and the personality on the page is not that of a father buckling under the strain. Doyle combines his unique voice with his optimistic, humorous point of view to give the reader not just a story, but a storyteller who compels us to stick around and see what happens next.

⊞ THE BOOK DOCTOR MAKES A HOUSE CALL
The Cure for Common Problems with Voice and Point of View

It is never just what you say. Equally important is how you say it.

So clear your throat and get started.

❶ DIAGNOSIS: Your Voice Is Too Soft or Too Scratchy

A voice too soft, too indistinct, or one that shifts, careens, hits false notes, and can't quite find its true center, is often the result of an author's lack of confidence. "Can I really talk that way in my writing? What would Mrs. Garfield, my high school English teacher, say?"

Problems like these are normal and to be expected in early drafts, especially if you are new to the task of writing at book length. Don't despair, but don't neglect to address the issue either.

⬛▷ THE CURE

Before you can bring your real voice to your writing, you may need to rediscover it. We are, after all, trained to leave idiosyncrasies of speech and personality out of essays and research papers when we are in school, and we are likewise trained to keep unique words and phrases out of the memos and reports we produce if we write at work, so it is easy to lose track. Is it time, perhaps, to remind yourself how you really sound?

Here are some questions to start you off:

1. Recall a saying that was common to an adult figure in your childhood. For instance, my mother often said, when she was at the end of her rope:

   What do you kids want, the shirt off my back?

   Or when I was sick, she would write a note to the school principal—though no one in my family ever played golf that I know of—saying:

   Dinty was not feeling up to par yesterday.

   Think also of your grandparents, and what sayings and unique similes or metaphors they brought with them from the previous generation. If you are lucky enough to have known great-grandparents or great-aunts or -uncles, try to remember how they spoke as well.

   Come up with as many as you can, write them down, and revisit the list every few days to see what else pops into your mind.

2. How would your mother, or grandmother, describe people in the town where you lived, or in the neighborhood?

   For instance:

   She thinks she sits at the right hand of God.

   He was born in a bottle.

You could eat your dinner off of her kitchen floor.

_____

_____

_____

3. Did your family or community have their own peculiar ways of expressing these common phrases:

. . . wrong side of the tracks?

_____

. . . dumb as dirt.

_____

. . . mean as all hell.

_____

. . . a real snake.

_____

What are some others?

_____

4. Where did you grow up? On isolated Illinois farmland, like Lee Martin? In Oil City, Pennsylvania? On Polish Hill? Near Put-in-Bay?

What words or phrases are common to the place you live or where you were raised?

_____

_____

_____

Perhaps you are thinking, *Gee, that's great for some folks, but where I grew up wasn't that interesting.* Well, even cookie-cutter suburbia has its own language:

Cul-de-sac

Park and ride

Strip mall

So don't give up so easily.

5. In the interview of Lee Martin cited on page 103, Martin further explains how the world of farming and farms became central to his voice and point of view:

> My characters, then, can never be separated from their landscapes. They define themselves in the way they act within, or respond to, those natural worlds. A man spends his days driving a tractor up and down a field, and he feels every bump and cut of that ground until he takes it in and his living takes on its rhythm. A man like Mr. Dees watches the purple martins swoop and dart above a flat land that stretches out to the horizon, and he starts to think about what holds him in place and what threatens to leave him untethered.[15]

What is it about the landscape surrounding the people in your novel or memoir that defines them, that becomes a part of their inner rhythm? (Remember, every location has a landscape, not just the rural ones. Cities, suburbs, even high school hallways and prison blocks have their own landscapes.)

_____

_____

_____

6. Now think of a story from your childhood, the sort of story that someone will always bring up eventually if you get together with your brothers and sisters and talk late into the night. Perhaps a funny story, or a melancholy one. (If you are an only child, or if the prospect of getting together with your siblings makes you cringe, feel free to substitute a cousin or best childhood friend.)

Once the story is clear in your mind, write it down, capturing as best you can the messy, rambling speech patterns that your friend or relative would use to tell it, pauses and sentence fragments and "ums" and "aahs" included.

_____

_____

_____

_____

_____

Once finished, "clean it up"—but just enough for it to make sense to a reader who isn't familiar with the story or your family.

Don't make it "correct." Let the oddities stay and save the peculiar turns of phrase.

❾ DIAGNOSIS: You Don't See So Well from Your Main Character's Point of View

Your job as author is to see the world from the viewpoint of your main character, as if you were in her skull looking out of her eye sockets, behind her eardrums hearing precisely the sounds that she hears, in her nasal passages smelling what she smells, and so forth, but also as if you were in her brain, processing and evaluating (and perhaps avoiding and rationalizing) just as she would.

But sometimes that is tough, and not only for novelists. Even memoirists may find it hard at times to understand the person they were twenty years ago. That long-ago you may seem like a stranger.

⇒ THE CURE

Understanding and empathy are fully required.

Remember that no one wakes up in the morning and thinks, "Gee, today I'll make choices that screw my life up but good." We all wake up planning to do well, or right those parts of our complicated lives that feel wrong. Even hardcore addicts are pretty sure that they'll quit using, "probably tomorrow."

Stop judging and try to understand the fears, the limitations, the confusion of your main character, or the younger you.

If that's not enough to make you feel comfortable and confident in your ability to capture the person on the page, interview people who resemble your character in some way, or find diaries and other records.

Remember that people are contradictions: if you are writing your character as someone who is consistently just one way, in thought *and* action, you are likely misunderstanding them.

Finally, consider writing certain scenes from the point of view of the antagonist—the person your main character is up against, either by working at cross-purposes with them or by directly butting heads. If you are writing from a limited point of view, these scenes won't ultimately make it into your novel or memoir, but they can be very helpful in understanding what the world looks like from each of two (or five) sides.

❸ DIAGNOSIS: There's Information You Need Your Reader to Understand, But Your Point-of-View Character Doesn't Know About It

Limited point of view can be frustrating. But so is real life.

▶ THE CURE

We are always operating in the dark in some manner. This is what makes life interesting; what keeps us alert, alive, and in anticipation.

It works the same way in storytelling. Traveling alongside your main character as he or she makes sense of the world, accumulates bits of knowledge, gathers clues to some unanswered question, is part of the joy of reading. You are not writing an instruction manual, you are writing a story, and true stories contain those moments when the main characters have no idea what is around the next corner, or sometimes no idea how they've landed in the very spot where they find themselves.

This is true of all memoir, of course. You are limited to what you know, what you imagine, and how you interpret. You can't ever truly be sure of a family member's motivations or rationalizations. You can hardly be sure of your own. Even if your sister "explains" the reason she married her first husband, despite the fact that everyone thought at the time that he was a complete bum, all you really know now is her *current* explanation. Even if it is her intention to be entirely honest with you, memory is slippery, and perception changes over time.

In fiction, your main character may not yet be able to grasp that the cell phone calls her husband insists on answering out on the back deck and his long "golf weekends" clearly signal an extramarital affair, but your reader, with the distance that comes from being outside of the relationship, may begin to smell a rat early (and will await further clues with anticipatory pleasure).

Think of limited point of view as an opportunity to make your book real. Tell us what your character doesn't know or fails to understand. Or better yet, show us, through her words and actions, or through the actions of others, that she fails to properly understand.

PROMPTS AND EXERCISES TO CURE VOICE AND POINT-OF-VIEW PROBLEMS

As any honest doctor will tell you, regular exercise is essential to a healthy writing body.

THE LITERARY MIMIC

Your style and personality is not that of Ernest Hemingway, Joan Didion, or Brian Doyle. We are all different, and we all will ultimately speak and write in a different voice.

But temporary mimicry is not a bad idea. Think of it as stretching exercises, a way of forming stronger and more flexible narrative muscles.

Even J. K. Rowling is on board with this one: "You'll go through a phase where you will imitate your favorite writers and that's fine because that's a learning experience too."[16]

So the Book Doctor is prescribing the following exercise regimen:

Take the opening paragraph of your novel or memoir, or the opening of a chapter, and rewrite it, first with Hemingway's blunt sentences and one-syllable descriptors, and then as Didion might, with the questioning nature and tentative ideas that loop back and reexamine themselves. Then, try Brian Doyle's long (deliberately run-on) sentences full of skipping and tumbling phraseology.

Once that's completed, let Pip's sarcasm (from Dickens's *Great Expectations*) sneak into your prose.

Don't stop there. Go back to your own favorite writers and try to sound a bit like them. What makes Vonnegut sound like Vonnegut? How about Toni Morrison? Or Mary Karr?

In the end, the goal is not to be a copycat, but playing around like this is an excellent way of reminding yourself that there is more than one way to do anything.

WHAT WE KNOW WE KNOW, WHAT WE KNOW WE DON'T KNOW, AND WHAT WE DON'T KNOW WE DON'T KNOW

I am, I admit, paraphrasing a former secretary of defense in the title for this prompt, but perhaps it is best to set aside politics before we become too distracted.

An excellent way to more deeply understand the point of view of your main character (even if it is an earlier incarnation of you, the author) is to answer these three questions:

1. What is it about the situation that your character does not know?
2. What is it that your character thinks he knows, but he is dead wrong (and won't know this until later)?
3. What will your character never know?

If your character, or the memoir-drawn you, understands everything about the situation, about himself, and about the world he lives in, then he can't be very real, can he?

["Prose is architecture,
not interior decoration . . ."

—ERNEST HEMINGWAY[1]]

6 | THE STRONG SKELETON

PLOT AND STRUCTURE

Let's talk about bones for a moment. In case you haven't noticed, they are pretty much what holds us together.

Novels and memoirs have bones as well, or they should, and any good Book Doctor will tell you that keeping a healthy skeleton is as important in the literary arena as it is in the personal.

Otherwise, everything just sags.

So what is a skeleton, where books are concerned? A book's skeleton is a combination of plot and structure, two related but separate ways of looking at story, both of them essential to keeping each and every page of your book properly aligned.

What Is Plot?

Plot grows directly out of the story of your book (the heart story discussed in chapter 1), but instead of the all-encompassing Hero's Journey, a plot is made up of individual events, discrete stops along the extended trail.

So for instance, the central story of a novel or memoir might be the narrator's struggle to overcome a childhood marked by extreme poverty and the low expectations his teachers and parents have for him. Harrison, as we'll call him, loves to draw, and he begins to sense that he might have more potential than others are willing to recognize. His journey in the book will be to discover for himself if he does, indeed, have real talent, and then prove his worth to others, despite continuing self-doubts and additional obstacles in his way.

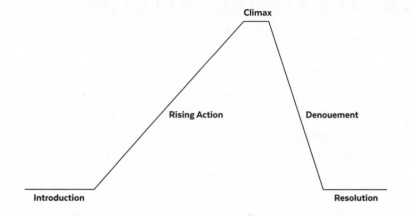

In visual terms, the sketch above is an overly simplified but still useful illustration often used to demonstrate how plot works over the course of a story.

The introduction is just that, though I highly advise you keep any introductory material as brief as possible, or do away with it completely. (See "In Media Res" in the structure discussion on page 130.)

The rising action is the day-to-day or year-to-year climb toward some goal (or away from some unwanted situation), with small and large obstacles along the path. It is also important to note that effective plots have causality; the obstacles are not random, but are the result of the novel's main character or the memoir's first-person author attempting to reach the goal or avoid the calamity.

The climax is the make-or-break moment—an instant in time when the hero is teetering on the edge, with success on one side and failure on the other. (Depending on the tone or genre of the book, the "teetering moment" may be every bit as dramatic as it seems or it may be subtler, perhaps spiritual or psychological.)

The denouement (from a French word meaning "to untie") are the events immediately after the teetering moment, as the narrator or main character's world settles into a new normal.

The resolution is life going on, as it always does.

So for instance, in our hypothetical story, the rising action begins with Harrison's internal struggle: the voices of his teachers, even his parents, suggesting he is not smart enough, not likely to succeed. Harrison, however, has begun (cautiously, at least) to believe in himself and his abilities. Perhaps on a practical level he decides what he needs is to leave his mediocre urban high school and transfer to a magnet school where he can enroll in serious art classes. This opening action is followed by the resistance of his school's small-minded principal and the weak support of his parents—"Why would anyone want to study art?"

Through perseverance, Harrison, now in his junior year, manages to have his transfer to the better school approved, and in subsequent chapters—though obstacles continue to arise—Harrison wins an award for his drawings, meets teachers who recognize his talent, and eventually, in his senior year, is accepted into a good college with a strong program in the visual arts.

Except, wait one moment: How will he pay his college tuition? Here's a major setback. All Harrison has worked for seems lost, until . . . well, there are any number of ways this obstacle might propel the book forward. Perhaps Harrison gives up his dream for a while and sinks back into doubt and despondency. The reader is despondent too, because by this time we care about the young artist. The pattern of rising and falling action would continue, with setbacks, advances, and false starts, until Harrison's drawings begin to attract enough interest that a local gallery owner takes them on. The work begins to sell.

In this hypothetical book, the climax might occur years into the future, when Harrison has his first showing in a well-regarded Manhattan art gallery. Perhaps another obstacle pops up here: Harrison's self-doubts return, or he has an enemy in the art community, motivated by jealousy, slurring his reputation with whispered innuendo. In the book, we hold our breath as Harrison waits to see if anyone shows up at the gallery opening, as he overhears comments from people filing past his drawings and paintings, and, in the days and weeks to follow, as he waits expectantly to see if the major art magazines run reviews of his work.

Let's say it all turns out well: his work is admired, well-reviewed, and purchased by influential collectors. The brief denouement might give us a sense of how Harrison handles this well-earned success, his newfound confidence, and a growing sense of purpose. The conclusion might show Harrison deciding that it is now his mission to help younger artists chart their own course, putting together educational programs so children from his inner-city neighborhood have opportunities he never had.

What I just gave you, of course, is a summary, lacking full characterization, setting, scene, intimate detail, sensory description, voice, or point of view. The plot is only a small part of the equation. These other elements—detailed characterization and the rest—are what ensure that readers care about Harrison's setbacks and advances, that they suffer his disappointments and share in his accomplishments along the way. While plot is important, don't fool yourself that a good plot is all that one needs.

One way to think about plot is that it's the storyline, what a reader might tell a friend when recommending the book: *There is this kid named Harrison, and he comes from this awful neighborhood in Trenton, New Jersey, but he can draw, and has dreams of being an accomplished artist, yet that's easier said than done when his teachers and his own family dismiss his talent, so he tries to change schools . . .*

So, What Is Structure?

Structure is to your book what architecture is to a building.

Consider this: If every house in the world were made of red brick, with a central doorway on the ground level, front steps flanked by small bushes, a rectangular window on both sides of the doorway, and a peaked roof, it would be a very dull world (and many of us would regularly walk into the wrong house when returning home late in the evening).

But houses exist in a seemingly infinite range of designs, and that goes for books as well.

Some books tell the central story fairly straightforwardly, while others experiment in small or large ways. The important move here, of course, is to be aware of your options.

CHRONOLOGICAL

A chronological structure presents events in the order in which they occurred, moving sequentially through time from where the story begins to where it all wraps up. For instance, Dickens's *David Copperfield* begins at his birth—"To begin my life with the beginning of my life, I record that I was born . . ."[2]—and follows him from childhood all the way on to adulthood. A chronological narrative needn't begin at birth of course, unless you have good reason to. A better strategy is to begin at the moment the story becomes particularly interesting.

FRAME, OR BOOKEND

Zora Neale Hurston's *Their Eyes Were Watching God* begins and ends with two main characters, Janie and Pheoby, sitting on a porch, as Janie tells stories to Pheoby during the course of an evening. The stories that Janie shares comprise the narrative of the novel, nestled within the frame or bookends of the one night of storytelling.

IN MEDIA RES

Here, the story begins "in the midst of things," with the author filling in any necessary background story later on in the book. Cheryl Strayed's memoir *Wild* begins with Strayed standing above the treetops, on a rock ledge atop a mountain in Northern California.

"Moments before," she writes, "I'd removed my hiking boots and the left one had fallen into those trees, first catapulting into the air when my enormous backpack toppled onto it, then skittering across the gravelly trail and flying over the edge. It bounced off a rocky outcropping several feet beneath me before disappearing into the forest canopy below, impossible to retrieve."[3]

She could have started at the beginning of her epic hike, or even years earlier when her life began to unravel, but this moment—literally a precipice—hooks the readers from both directions:

How did she get there?

How will she ever proceed without her left boot?

SEGMENTED

The events in Toni Morrison's *The Bluest Eye* are arranged in sections titled Autumn, Winter, Spring, and Summer, and contain separate blocks of narration, alternating between various characters and a third-person narrator. As readers, we put the pieces together as we read.

BRAIDED

Benjamin Percy's *Red Moon* follows a number of characters over the course of years, alternating between the characters with intertwining narrative strands. Think of a pigtail, each strand of the braid representing a separate narrative, but all connected, a part of the whole.

BACKWARD

Martin Amis's novel *Time's Arrow* is a bit of a tour de force. The novel recounts the life of a German doctor, but told in reverse chronology, because this is how the main character experiences life. Amis bases this unique structure on a concept from physics asserting that the arrow of time moves simultaneously in both directions.

Charles Baxter employs a backward narrative as well, in his novel *First Light*, but his book does not rely on physics. He simply starts the story of his two main characters, brother and sister Hugh and Dorsey Welch, well into their adult years, and then moves backward through time to Dorsey's birth, and the moment that Hugh touches his newborn sister's hand for the first time.

EPISTOLARY

Stephen Chbosky's coming-of-age novel *The Perks of Being a Wallflower* offers a series of letters written by a fifteen-year-old boy named Charlie to an unknown recipient. Helen Fielding's *Bridget Jones's Diary*, not surprisingly, is told through a series of fictional diary entries. Bram Stoker's *Dracula* is told through a series of letters, diary entries, and ship's log entries.

Of course, this is the twenty-first century, so novels and memoirs are also appearing in new epistolary modes, such as tweets, emails, and Facebook postings. Jennifer Egan even added PowerPoint slides to her novel *A Visit from the Goon Squad*.

EXPERIMENTAL

All good writing is an experiment, ultimately, and even the most straightforward mode of storytelling may exist because the author experimented with a number of innovative structures before trying out, and choosing, the chronological approach.

But some books employ structures that seem to have been designed specifically for the story being told. Marcia Aldrich modeled her memoir *Companion to an Untold Story* on a reference book, presenting a series of alphabetized entries listing objects and memories left behind when a close friend committed suicide. In *Body Geographic*, Barrie Jean Borich employs a series of maps—real, imagined, metaphorical—to explore the migration of her Croatian ancestors, her own midwestern roots, her body, her tattoos, her relationships, and the various "landscapes of memory"[4] in her life.

This is not an exhaustive list, by any means, and even if it were, some author is even now inventing yet one more new way to structure a novel or memoir.

It is natural, of course, for writers to want to know early on—or to ask their writing coach, workshop leader, or Book Doctor to tell them—which is the best approach for the book they are writing. Unfortunately, no one can really tell you, and in most cases you will need to undergo time-consuming (but instructive) months of trial and error.

There are no shortcuts, though it certainly helps to read as many books as you possibly can, and to take note (mentally or in an actual notebook) of how various authors have tackled the challenge of structure. The best memoirs read like novels, and some of the best novels seem entirely real, so dipping into both genres is good practice.

And keep in mind the advice of Douglas Adams, author of *The Hitchhiker's Guide to the Galaxy* and the four other novels that make up his five-book "trilogy":

> I rarely end up where I was intending to go, but often I end up somewhere I needed to be.[5]

⊞ THE BOOK DOCTOR MAKES A HOUSE CALL

The Cure for Common Problems with Plot and Structure

When your skeleton is hurting, it is time to see the chiropractor. Consider these "manipulations" designed to snap your book's structure into proper alignment.

❷ DIAGNOSIS: People Say the Plot Seems Forced and Predictable

Well, my first question would be: Which people? Be careful of the advice you get, and the criticism you heed, until you know whether the source of that advice is knowledgeable and actually trying to help.

But let's assume more than one person has suggested your plot seems forced, too tidy, or contrived, and this constructive advice comes from folks you trust to know what they are saying. The problem with a forced or predictable plot is that real life more often than not is messy and irregular, so any story that seems otherwise is not going to ring true.

▰▷ THE CURE

Remember the words of Anne Lamott, who, like many authors, knows that the best plots spring from character: "I've always sort of believed that these people inside—these characters—know who they are and what they're about and what happens, and they need me to help get it down on paper because they don't type."[6]

If your plot takes predictable turns toward a foreseeable conclusion, or if the resolution of each obstacle on the path seems too straightforward, the problem may very well be that you have your hands on the main character's shoulders, pushing her along, forcing her to act the way *you need her to act* in order to finish your book, rather than letting her be herself.

That's never a good idea.

Playwright and fiction writer Romulus Linney once told me, "Never think 'What can I make my character do here that will be interesting?' Instead, once you've created a character, imbued him with a personality, given him various tendencies, and a past, ask yourself, 'What *would* he do, *really* do, given the situation at hand?'"

If your plot turns are all-too-foreseeable, the obstacles too easily toppled, go back to the character—and that might mean the earlier you, in the memoir—and ask yourself a series of honest questions:

- Given the situation, what *would* he do?

- What mistakes would he make?

- What is he avoiding?

- What is he afraid of?

- What does he expect to happen?

- Where is he dead wrong in his expectations?

- What outside forces are going to turn a foreseeable outcome into something volatile and erratic?

Then return to the story, scene by scene, and make his reactions irregular, untidy, and real.

❸ DIAGNOSIS: You Are Stalled on Structure, Dithering Away for Days and Days

Being stalled is not failure, but remaining mired in your indecision for too long certainly is.

There are certain times when sitting at your desk, fingers hovering inches above the keyboard, brow wrinkled, your brain churning madly (or sputtering along) as it attempts to grasp precisely where your book is going and how it might get there, can actually be quite productive. Sometimes stopping intentionally to think something through can open the door to an inspirational spark.

But if you've been turning the question over and over in your mind for days, or goodness, for weeks and months, you need to start writing. If you wait until you have the perfect answer and full understanding, you may still be laboring over chapter one ten years down the road.

⇒ THE CURE

Think of two or three possible ways to structure your book and choose one. Roll the dice if you have to. Then start writing.

Even if the structure you have chosen turns out to be the wrong choice, when you determine this later on you will at least have a hundred pages of scenes and details that you can salvage and reassemble.

The subject of radical revision comes up in the chapter to follow, but in my experience few authors are so lucky that they don't occasionally have to rip out the seams and start over.

✎ PROMPTS AND EXERCISES TO CURE PLOT AND STRUCTURE PROBLEMS

At times you need to work on your project at the sentence level, refining every detail, improving every phrase. At other times, however, you need to step back and take in the whole picture. These prompts are designed to help you with the latter approach.

STILL STUCK ON PLOT?

Your heart story has to come from you. Whatever longing or aspiration drives your novel or memoir, it has to be flowing from your heart, your soul, or your gizzard. (Yes, like real doctors, the Book Doctor remains unsure precisely where our deepest feelings reside.)

But remember that plots are often very similar: either a man (or woman) goes on a journey, or a stranger (or unforeseen turn of events) comes to town. Countless books and stories fit one or the other of these classic forms.

You might also reread chapter 1 for the discussion of Joseph Campbell's study of the classic Hero's Journey, and see which parts might fit the story you are attempting to tell: the "call to adventure" (which may also be interpreted as a "call to overcome crisis" if your novel or memoir centers around illness or other threats to well-being), entry into a "special world" of tasks and obstacles, and the eventual return to the new ordinary.

Of course, there are other places to find plots that might be fruitful for adaptation or variation, including the hundreds of myths and fairy tales from our planet's various lands and cultures.

"My aunt and my mother read to me when I was three from all the old Grimm fairy tales, Andersen fairy tales, and then all the Oz books as I was growing up," science-fiction great Ray Bradbury once explained. "So by the time when I was ten or eleven, I was just full to the brim with these, and the Greek myths, and the Roman myths. And then, of course, I went to Sunday school, and then you take in the Christian myths, which are all fascinating in their own way. . . . If I'm anything at all, I'm not really a science-fiction writer—I'm a writer of fairy tales and modern myths about technology."[7]

Stories are everywhere.

Try this:

1. List three or four of your favorite novels or memoirs.

2. Now go to your bookshelf, take them down, and refresh your memory. For each one, write a one-sentence description of what occurs. ("There is this kid named Harrison who wants to be an artist, but no one believes in him and he barely believes in himself . . ." or "A man named Ahab recruits a rough-edged crew to pursue a nemesis at sea . . .")

3. Now chart, broadly, the ups and downs of the major plot. What brings the narrator or main character closer to her goal? What gets in her way? How do these obstacles change as she gets closer to her stated objective? A full-length book might have hundreds of instances; focus on charting the major ones.

4. Now mark down next to these plot points where in the book they occur, by either chapter number or page number.

5. Pretend you are Harrison, the would-be artist, and get out the pencils. Try to *visually* approximate the ups and downs, the peaks and valleys, of each of these book-length plots. Drawer higher peaks for the major obstacles, deeper valleys for the major setbacks, and approximate in whatever way makes sense to you the distances in between.

6. Now do the same for the book you are working on.

7. No two books look exactly alike, and there is no unbreakable rule (other than, don't bore the reader with long stretches where *nothing* happens), but compare how the plot profile of your book looks visually next to the plot profiles of the three other books you have chosen.

8. Adjust accordingly.

STRUGGLING WITH STRUCTURE?

Consider Ben Percy's approach:

> Long before I begin writing, I rip a long sheet of paper from my children's art easel and hang it from my office wall and begin to brainstorm. I sketch out plot points. I draw and build histories and emotional arcs for characters. I know that some writers prefer a more organic process, but my own feeling is, you don't build a cathedral without a set of blueprints.
>
> Over the top of the blueprint, I sketch out a kind of cardiogram or seismograph in order to understand the spikes and dips in tension. I often move plot points around—sometimes withholding information for several chapters—in order to create different layers of tension and strategically organize explosive and revelatory moments.[8]

Percy is more proactive than many authors, but the approach he outlines is useful whether you start charting before you begin, as he does, or stop somewhere in the middle of your project to blueprint the "spikes and dips" of your book's structure.

Percy steals long sheets of paper from his children (who will probably forgive him someday). Other folks I've known use index cards, pinned to a corkboard or taped to the wall.

Or, if you've got a closet full of shoe boxes, you might label them chapter one, chapter two, chapter three, and so on, and drop slips of paper representing major and minor turning points, key scenes, and new obstacles into the appropriate boxes. Then try moving those slips of paper around, or even shifting the position of boxes, to see how that might advantageously alter how readers experience your story.

You could probably devise a similar scheme using different varieties of cookies—chocolate chip cookies represent one character, sugar cookies another, oatmeal raisin a third—and when they are stacked one atop the other, the cookie pile represents who is in the particular scene. Major developments might be marked by cupcakes.

Maybe that isn't a good idea.

Maybe the Book Doctor just needs lunch.

The idea, though, is to find a method to replicate structure in some useful visual way, one that reminds you that until your book is printed and on the shelves, nothing is set in stone.

Part II

CHECKUPS

"I write entirely to find out what I'm thinking, what I'm looking at, what I see and what it means."

—JOAN DIDION[1]

7 | KEEPING FIT

MOVING FROM FIRST DRAFT TO FIFTEENTH DRAFT

It is time, I'm afraid, for more tough medicine from the Book Doctor. To be entirely honest, this might hurt a little, and I apologize, but it is for your own good.

Here we go:

Once you are done writing your book, you aren't really done writing your book.

Yes, I understand. Being reminded of just how much effort is required even after you've put a period on the final sentence of the final chapter can be downright discouraging.

Revision does take effort and time.

It needn't, however, be painful.

The truth is, revision is my favorite part of writing. The blank page can be frightening. A few hundred or a few thousand words, on the other hand, pointing in the right direction but in need of some tender loving care, can be exhilarating. Words are like clay—you can push them around and make all sorts of different shapes with them. And clay reminds me of childhood. And childhood reminds me of the time when I was the most playful, most creative, and least haunted by voices telling me I can't do things well enough.

Perhaps it is just a trick of the mind, but here is what works for me:

- You can approach revision with your head low and your shoulders tensed, thinking, "Boy my sentences are so sloppy and wordy and I don't write nearly as well as I wish that I could, and all in all I'm a pathetic failure."

- Or you can approach revision thinking, "Hey, here's my chance to get it right. Let's start playing around."

How many times have you walked away from a difficult discussion as your brain swirled with all the things you should have said and how you might have made certain points more forcefully? Too many areas of life don't afford you a second chance, but writing does, and I highly recommend you see that as a good thing.

Now, for the playful part.

One of the best pieces of advice I received as a young writer came from the novelist David Bradley, who outlined exactly how to approach revision at each stage of a work, draft one to draft fifteen. He reminded me, and other writing students in the room, that we have inside our heads at least three distinct modes of self-evaluation.

The first is the Child mode. As kids, sitting on the kitchen floor, gifted with three lumps of colorful Play-Doh—blue, red, and yellow are the only colors I remember—our first instinct is to just fool around. Roll the first lump between your palms and make a snake. Bend the snake around to make a wreath or a bagel. Smoosh that bagel into a solid disk and use one of the other colors to make eyes, a nose, and a mouth. Voilà! You've got a goofy clay face.

And on and on and on. The only goal is to see what can be done. No judgment, just pure experimentation and delight.

This, Bradley told us, should be where we are, the mode we employ, in our first to third drafts of a project, large or small. Let's just see what can be done with this idea or story. Let's slap as much of it down on the page as we can and then step back a bit to admire the mess we've made. Let's get our hands dirty and maybe our knees as well. Worries are for grown-ups.

Which brings us to the Adult mode.

Somewhere along the way, we have to make the switch. The equation is slightly different for every writer; my first and second drafts are sloppy, loosely crafted, trial-and-error sorts of messes, whereas other successful writers I know spend more time on their initial drafts and come out of the first round with something far more solid and respectable. Every writer has to find her own pace.

Eventually—for me it is more like draft three—the Adult voice enters the conversation, asking practical question like:

Is this worth spending more time on?

Exactly where are we headed here?

What will it take to reach my goal?

Am I giving the reader enough?

How do I make this better?

Adults have to pay the rent, and buy groceries. They tend to be less spirited and improvisational than children (and often, less fun to be around). But adults do come in handy, and without them, probably no book would ever really reach completion.

The final mode, then, is Parent, the voice that notices every little flaw, and one that often chides and scolds. Imagine your mother questioning your new hairstyle, or asking if your outfit is really appropriate for church. Or imagine your father critiquing your lawn-mowing technique.

In terms of writing, the Parent mode voice sounds a bit like this:

My goodness, that's one convoluted sentence.

Did you mean to write it that way?

Oh come on, that scene goes on for three pages and nothing ever happens.

You just used the word "it" four times in two sentences.

That's the best metaphor you've got?

Though the exacting Parent voice pointing out every flaw in our sentences and each weakness in our word choices tries to push itself in at every stage of writing, what Bradley taught me through his three-stage illustration is to ignore this hypercritical voice, until the end. And to then give it my total attention.

Listening to that chiding voice too early, in the first couple of drafts, just leads to despondency and chronic writer's block. But not listening to it at the very end, not letting your most critical side reflect on whether the story, chapter, or book is ready to go out to an agent or editor, or to readers, is a mistake as well.

Each of the three modes—Child, Adult, Parent—is useful, at the proper stage. Learning to control them can make the entire process of writing and revision more pleasant, and more fruitful.

Exercising Smartly: Some Tips on Healthy Revision

Thoughtful revision takes varied forms, from sentence level to story level, with different considerations and questions at every stage.

The first crucial distinction, however, is that revision is entirely separate from proofreading. Checking the accuracy of your spelling, typing, verb tenses, and so on is vital, but not a substitute for serious, substantive manuscript review.

So let's say you have finished your first draft, or second, and it is time to honestly evaluate your own work.

Here is how to proceed.

FIRST: GO BACK TO THE BEGINNING

Once you have found an ending to your novel or memoir, the point where the story concludes (not wrapped up too neatly, not extended out into infinity, but a point of resolution and new balance), take a good look at your opening impulse. These two moments should be connected, either by a direct line of action and reaction running through your entire story, or through the current of emotion. Sometimes these two moments may also be linked by setting, by imagery, through a recurrent metaphor, or through framing or other structural techniques. There is no steadfast rule, except that if the beginning and ending don't feel coupled in any significant way, you need to rethink plot and structure.

Another way to look at this is to remind yourself that a book begins with a question: "How will she overcome this unforeseen challenge?" or "Will this experience change him in some significant way?"

The ending doesn't always answer the question fully, but it should connect, and though the beginning often doesn't ask the question explicitly, it should plant the seed.

THEN: EVERYTHING IN THE MIDDLE

Yes, *everything.*

Remember the Invisible Magnetic River introduced in chapter 1? Identifying this Invisible River flowing underneath your story is enormously useful when the time comes for serious, effective revision. There are scenes you possibly labored over for days that may no longer have any utility to the story, or images and metaphors that—though not poorly shaped—don't fit the overall flow. Even entire chapters may prove to be superfluous— and though it is heart-breaking to delete twenty pages of honest effort, this momentary agony is far more desirable than settling for a book that limps or sputters somewhere midway.

Locate the emotional undercurrent of your book and review every word, image, metaphor, scene, character, and chapter. If these elements are not connected to the River, not sharing the magnetic pull, then grab your scissors (or make use of the delete key).

To use a film metaphor, knowing the root story, the emotional undercurrent, the heart of it all, allows the author to know precisely where to point the narrative camera, how long to keep the camera rolling, and when to yell "Cut!"

FINALLY: THE SENTENCE LEVEL

This part is the most fun for me, honestly, though perhaps I have an odd sense of what is enjoyable. In any case, reading the manuscript through from beginning to end, every sentence, one at a time, OUT LOUD, is an opportunity I relish.

Remember, the best approach goes like this: *Hey, here's my chance to get it right. Let's start playing around.*

Listening to each sentence, feeling it inside of my mouth as I speak it, identifying words I use too often, finding phrases that seem flat, asking if what I'm saying is actually what I mean, is an opportunity I don't have in everyday life, in spoken conversation. Getting it right feels good.

Often I improve a sentence the same way I review it, by speaking it out loud, and then trying another pattern, substituting another word, and speaking the revised sentence out loud. My ear is frequently more helpful than my brain in identifying simple awkwardness and also in recognizing the more vexing problem of sentences that sound good but say little.

I don't mean to be overly Suzie Sunshine here. There are days that rewriting can be a slog, just as writing can be. There are moments in revision that I think I'll never find the solution, moments of despair and discouragement.

But overall the process is invigorating, and when working well, invigorating for both my prose *and* my story.

I've been lucky enough to publish a dozen books, along with hundreds of short stories, essays, and articles. I don't think for a moment that I'm smarter than other people, and I don't think I was born with better ideas. What I do think is that I revise to a greater extent than many who give up too soon.

The difference, in my mind, between writers who are successful in finding an audience and those who struggle, is when and where in the revision process a writer throws in the towel and settles for "good enough." Learn to be just a bit tougher on your own work than the toughest editor you can imagine, and you just might find that editors suddenly love your work.

"And by the way, everything in life is writable about if you have the outgoing guts to do it, and the imagination to improvise. The worst enemy to creativity is self-doubt."

—SYLVIA PLATH[1]

8 | AN APPLE A DAY

HEALTHY HABITS FOR ANY WRITER

Yes, the Book Doctor loves to diagnose and cure story problems, and yes, he is a seemingly endless font of advice (cue the eye rolls from family and friends), but what would really be terrific is if you could keep your writing practice healthy on your own and avoid seeing the Doctor altogether.

Remember, writing a book doesn't have to be painful, even though it is challenging, and if the writing does become painful, there is a good chance that we are bringing the misery on ourselves. So consider these positive steps to improve your overall authorial well-being, and don't forget to eat your fruits and vegetables.

Show Up

Isabel Allende thought this bit of advice important enough to say it three times:

> Show up, show up, show up, and after a while the muse shows up, too.[2]

Richard Bausch goes a step further:

> Be patient. You are trying to do something that is harder than just about anything there is to do, even when it feels easy. You will write many more failures than successes. Say to yourself, 'I accept failure as the condition of this life, this work. I freely accept it as my destiny.' Then go on and do the work.[3]

My version goes like this:

> I still have bad days, sometimes strings of bad days, when
> it feels as if I'm just pushing my pencil back and forth,
> trying to pull workable words from an empty well. But I've
> convinced myself over the years that I have to continue
> sitting at my desk through these bad days, checking
> them off as "completed" on some invisible chart, before
> the good days suddenly come rolling in, days when my
> thoughts are firing more quickly than my fingers can
> capture them, days when up to 60 percent of what I type
> is, with a good bit of revision, absolutely useful to the
> final draft.

If I allowed myself to get up from the desk and go watch *Law
& Order* any time it felt as if my muse was not in attendance, I'd
be a guy who can recite every *Law & Order* episode from memory
rather than a guy who writes books.

This philosophy has served me well, and I think it will serve
you well too.

Show up.

Stick around.

The words will come.

Study Your Craft

As choreographer Twyla Tharp once observed, "The great painters
are incomparable draftsmen. They also know how to mix their own
paint, grind it, put in the fixative. . . . A great chef can chop and
dice better than anyone in the kitchen. The best fashion designers
are invariably virtuosos with a needle and thread."[4]

And the best writers know words, know sentences, understand
how rhythm works, how metaphor deepens, how a story can be

formulaic or a story can be nuanced, unpredictable, and real. The best writers listen constantly to how words *sound*, to how reversing the order of sentences or clauses also reverses how a reader processes what is read, and to how a long sentence creates one effect while a very abrupt sentence can create another.

Entirely.

The best writers also read promiscuously, analyze what they've read, and discuss what they've read with other thoughtful writers. The best writers attempt constantly to learn from how other storytellers have constructed their stories, including those stories written by seeming geniuses and those stories that somehow entirely miss the mark. The best writers constantly ask, "Why? Why did this work while that went splat?"

You can hone your craft right at home, in a chair, holding a book, a notebook, or a keyboard. You can also, if time and money allow, take classes at your local literary center or community college. Writing classes can't teach creativity, of course, but they can help you to improve various techniques and assist with revision strategies.

Depending on where you live, there may be a weekly or monthly writers' group offering critique, discussion, and community. Often, these group meetings are hosted at bookstores, or at the public library.

Also useful are the growing number of weekend or weeklong workshops and conferences. A benefit of these events is that there are other nice people in attendance, many of them also tackling a first novel or memoir, and it helps to make contact with folks who will commiserate with you when the writing goes poorly and celebrate with you when the writing goes well.

And often, there is wine at the end of the day.

It doesn't matter how you do it, though, as long as you keep learning new ways to mix your own paint, grind it, and put in the fixative.

Ignore the Voices

Writer's block is a daunting term, calling to mind a thick wall constructed with weighty cement bricks, sitting smack dab between you and your writing. The truth, however, is that writer's block is actually made from something far less solid: those unremitting, whiny voices in our heads.

Mine regularly tell me "This is the stupidest idea any writer has ever had," or "You simply don't have the native intelligence or vocabulary to say anything smart," or, on a particularly bad day, "You're fat, you're stupid, your teeth are weird, and your nostrils are huge."

That last one may have been not a voice in my head, but rather the voice of my high school gym teacher. All the same, the voices are just voices, and not even real. Instead, they are transitory, self-manufactured electrical impulses jolting rudely through our neural pathways. Yet many of us waste countless hours, days, even years believing they are genuine, and letting them keep us from our goals.

It is wasted energy trying to turn them off, because the truth is, you never will.

Which leaves you two choices:

1. Listen to them. Stop writing. Hate yourself.

2. Write anyway. Smile sweetly at the voices and say back to them, "Okay, you're right, but I'm going ahead anyway."

It is amazing how much work a stupid writer with no good ideas and huge nostrils can get done if he just passes over the requisite thirty minutes of self-loathing and starts crafting sentences.

Endure

Sometimes we lose our way, either as writers or as writers trying to navigate a particular story.

Losing our way as a writer probably means we need to recharge our batteries, through travel, good books, a bit of rest, or sitting in a chair in the backyard reminding ourselves of why we do this in the first place. There is no shame in giving up, as long as you only give up for a few days.

Losing our way as we try to navigate a particular story, on the other hand, is just part of the equation, something that happens time and again, because writing is fundamentally hard to do well, and it gets even tougher when you tackle a project of significant length, such as a book. Two hundred to three hundred pages that connect beginning to end, with a graceful story arc, compelling characters, and key challenges and resolutions, all told in clear, and even better, beautiful language, is a hefty assignment.

Let's think of this for a moment in terms of cooking a meal:

To prepare a roasted chicken dinner, with mashed potatoes, and a side of seasonal vegetables, and to ensure that all three dishes arrive at the table piping hot, takes talent and coordination. Now imagine doing this for two hundred people, at a gala banquet, and instead of chicken and vegetables, you are responsible for a seven-course dinner—a delicate avocado soup, arugula salad with goat cheese, grilled zucchini and rosemary bruschetta, broiled sea bass, roasted parsnips with fennel, pepper-rubbed rack of lamb, and apricot gelato for dessert—each course involving multiple skills and intricate culinary techniques.

That's what writing a book is like.

So, take heart.

Realizing that you've come unmoored from your story somewhere in chapter three or chapter five, or finishing an entire draft and then throwing up your hands and crying, "Oh, cripes! I'm not even sure anymore what this book is about!" is not a sign of failure. It is, instead, evidence that you are attempting something extremely challenging, and in that attempt, mistakes are made.

They always are. In the kitchen. In building a small business. In raising children. In any endeavor worth tackling.

Let Thomas Edison offer the advice this time: "I have not failed 10,000 times. I have not failed once. I have succeeded in proving that those 10,000 ways will not work. When I have eliminated the ways that will not work, I will find the way that will work."[5]

Accept Rejection

It happens, to all of us. (And though I'm talking about writing and publishing here, not high school, believe me, high school was horrible too.)

The truth is that your work, or book proposal, or query letter, is likely to come back to you with a "No thank you" far more often than you'd like, but that unfortunately goes with the territory.

This is of crucial importance, however: It is not *you* being rejected. It is not even your ability as a writer being rejected. All that a rejection letter or email connotes is that a particular editor or agent, on a particular Tuesday or Friday afternoon, wasn't excited enough by what you sent to say "Yes, I want it." This could happen for any number of reasons, including exhaustion on the part of the editor, an agent who liked your idea but just saw one too similar, or simple conflicts in taste or aesthetics.

Consider this:

> Twenty-one publishers said no to William Golding's *Lord of the Flies*, a book that has gone on to sell more than 14.5 million copies.

C. S. Lewis reported that he had been rejected eight hundred times before selling his first story.

Alex Haley, author of *Roots*, wrote seven days a week for eight years before selling his first piece to a small magazine.

Tony Hillerman, author of the popular series of detective novels featuring the Navajo Tribal Police, was told early on, "If you insist on rewriting this, get rid of all that Indian stuff."[6]

An editor for the *San Francisco Examiner*, turning down an early story from Rudyard Kipling, wrote, "I'm sorry Mr. Kipling, but you just don't know how to use the English language."[7]

Louisa May Alcott, author of *Little Women*, was told, when she circulated her early work, to "stick to teaching."[8]

It seems that sometimes the gatekeepers get it wrong.

Explore

The world is capacious and enthralling, and whether you know it yet or not, you have more than one story to tell. We often begin by writing about ourselves and our life experiences, and there is nothing incorrect about that, but we writers need always to remain alert to other subjects, to all of the questions that pop up, large and small, and we need to consider whether these questions may lead us somewhere interesting.

Embrace the world.

That might mean traveling the planet, but it might also mean getting to know every plant, bird, and bug in your small backyard.

Be open, always.

In the words of novelist George Saunders, be "so open it hurts, and then open up some more."[9]

"We're dead as a species if we don't tell stories, because then we don't know who we are."

—ALAN RICKMAN[1]

9 | THE BOOK DOCTOR'S FINAL ILLEGIBLE SCRIBBLES

Yes, the Book Doctor wields a hefty prescription pad, and at times he can nag a bit about doing your daily sit-ups, but the key is to do what you can.

Each of us has to find our own pace.

Don't look back ten years from now, however, and think, "Oh well, I never found time for my writing. That's a real disappointment." Suppose you had devoted a mere one hour per week to your book over those ten years. That would amount to 520 hours. What could you have written in that time?

Even better, you'll likely find that the one hour per week stretches into two, or three, or more. Once your heart story, the primal question driving your project, comes alive, you'll *want* to continue writing. You'll find the time.

"If the doctor told me I had six minutes to live," Isaac Asimov once joked, "I'd type a little faster."[2]

Or maybe he wasn't joking?

But I'm a Book Doctor, not the type that gives you that sort of bad news. My hope here is that we all have ample years left to devote to our book project. And then even more years to tackle the next one.

The time has come to set this writing guide down and resume work on your book.

To that end, let me reiterate the three basics at the heart of the Story Cure:

1. Writing is painstaking, but it needn't be painful. If it *is* painful, look to the voices in your head, and tell them to shut up.

2. Find your story, that primal or heart story you need and want to tell. This story is what will sustain you through multiple drafts and countless hours of exploration.

3. When feeling stuck or discouraged, always return to story. The answers are there.

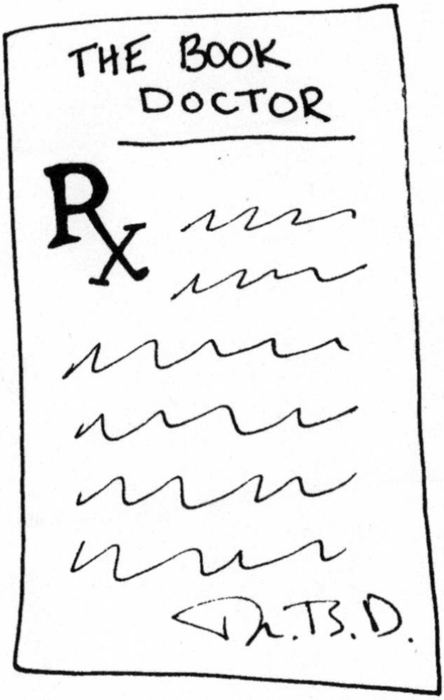
THE BOOK
DOCTOR
Rx
Dr. T.B.D.

Notes

1 | The Story Cure

1. Didion, Joan. *We Tell Ourselves Stories in Order to Live* (New York: Knopf, 2006), 185.

2. Lopez, Barry. "A Beginning: The Origins of Storytelling," *Poets & Writers*, Jan/Feb 2016, 48.

3. Percy, Benjamin. "Taking a Knife to the Nerve of the Moment: An Interview with Benjamin Percy," *Nothing But Comics*, March 3, 2015. https://nothingbutcomics.net/2015/03/03/percy/

4. Percy, Benjamin. *Red Moon* (New York: Grand Central Publishing, 2014), 53.

5. Strayed, Cheryl, quoted in Vicky Ferrier, "A Road Less Travelled: How Do You 'Just Be'?" *Lifeshifter*, Sept. 11, 2015. http://content.lifeshifter.com/article/VfHxvR0AAB4AxGWw/a-road-less-travelled-how-do-you-just-be

6. Vonnegut, Kurt. *Bagombo Snuff Box: Uncollected Short Fiction* (New York: G.P. Putnam's Sons, 1999), 9.

7. Hughes, Langston. *The Collected Poems of Langston Hughes* (New York: Knopf, 1994), 23.

8. Conrad, Joseph. *The Nigger of the Narcissus* (Garden City, NY: Doubleday & Co., 1914), 11.

9. Allende, Isabel. "Why I Write," in *Why We Write: 20 Acclaimed Authors on How and Why They Do What They Do*, ed. Meredith Maran (New York: Plume, 2013), 4.

10. Atchity, Kenneth. *A Writer's Time* (New York: W. W. Norton, 1986), 114.

2 | Your First Breath

1. Rushdie, Salman, quoted in "The Art of Fiction," in *The Paris Review Interviews III*, ed. Philip Gourevitch (New York: Picador, 2008), 379.

2. Gilbert, Elizabeth. *Eat, Pray, Love: One Woman's Search for Everything* (New York: Penguin, 2006), 7.

3. Picoult, Jodi. *My Sister's Keeper* (New York: Atria Books, 2004), 3.

4. Chandler, Raymond. *The Big Sleep* (New York: Pocket Books, 1950), 1.

5. Eugenides, Jeffrey. *The Virgin Suicides* (New York: Farrar, Straus and Giroux, 1993), 1.

6. Wolff, Tobias. *This Boy's Life* (New York: Grove Press, 1989), 3.

7. Austen, Jane. *Pride and Prejudice* (New York: Charles Scribner's Sons, 1918), 1.

8. Dickens, Charles. *David Copperfield* (New York: G.W. Carleton & Co., 1885), 9.

9. Bulwer-Lytton, Sir Edward. *Paul Clifford* (Philadelphia: J. B. Lippincott & Co., 1866), 17.

10. L'Engle, Madeleine. *A Wrinkle in Time* (New York: Farrar, Straus and Giroux, 2009), 7.

11. Singer, Issac Bashevis, quoted in "The Art of Fiction," in *The Paris Review Interviews II*, ed. Philip Gourevitch (New York: Picador, 2007), 98.

12. King, Stephen, quoted in Joe Fassler, "Why Stephen King Spends 'Months and Even Years' Writing Opening Sentences," Atlantic.com, July 2013. www.theatlantic.com/entertainment/archive/2013/07/why-stephen-king-spends-months-and-even-years-writing-opening-sentences/278043

13. Heat-Moon, William Least. *Blue Highways* (New York: Houghton Mifflin, 1991), 3.

14. Karr, Mary. *The Liars' Club* (New York: Penguin Classics, 2015), 3.

15. Salinger, J. D. *The Catcher in the Rye* (New York: Back Bay Books, 2001), 3.

16. Camus, Albert. *The Stranger* (New York: Knopf/Everyman's Library, 1993), 3.

17. Fitzgerald, F. Scott. *The Great Gatsby* (New York: Charles Scribner's Sons, 1925), 1.

18. Sabatini, Rafael. *Scaramouche* (Boston: Houghton Mifflin, 1921), 3.

3 | Prescription for Healthy Prose

1. Lamott, Anne, quoted in Susan Wittig Albert, *An Extraordinary Year of Ordinary Days* (Austin: University of Texas Press, 2010), 173.

2. Leonard, Elmore. *Elmore Leonard's 10 Rules of Writing* (New York: William Morrow, 2007), 23.

3. Steinbeck, John, quoted in "Writers at Work," in *The Paris Review Interviews*, 4th Series, ed. George Plimpton (New York: Penguin Books, 1977), 186.

4. Dickens, Charles. *A Christmas Carol* (Oxford: Benediction Classics, 2012), 7.

5. Fitzgerald, *The Great Gatsby*, 9–10.

6. Gardner, John. *The Art of Fiction* (New York: Vintage Books, 1991), 203.

4 | The Lifeblood Test

1. Hamby, Barbara. "An Interview with Barbara Hamby," *storySouth*, February 11, 2007. www.storysouth.com/poetry_features/2007/02/an_interview_with_barbara_hamby.html

2. Bergen, Benjamin K., quoted in "Imagine a Flying Pig: How Words Take Shape in the Brain," *Morning Edition, NPR News*, May 2, 2013. www.npr.org/templates/transcript/transcript.php?storyId=180036711

3. Conrad, Joseph. *The Nigger of the Narcissus* (Garden City, NY: Doubleday & Co., 1914), 14.

4. Conrad, Joseph. *Heart of Darkness* (Boston: Bedford/St. Martin's, 2011), 53–54.

5. Ibid., 54.

6. Ibid., 53–54.

7. Ibid., 53–54.

8. Stevenson, Robert Louis. *Treasure Island* (Boston: Roberts Brothers, 1884), 10–12.

9. Prose, Francine. *Reading Like a Writer: A Guide for People Who Love Books and for Those Who Want to Write Them* (New York: Harper Perennial, 2006), 15–16.

5 | A Visit with the Throat and Eye Doctors

1.   King, quoted in Joe Fassler, "Why Stephen King Spends 'Months and Even Years' Writing Opening Sentences."

2.   Hemingway, Ernest. *A Farewell to Arms* (New York: Scribner, 2014), 3.

3.   Didion, Joan. *The Year of Magical Thinking* (New York: Knopf, 2006), 3–4.

4.   Baldwin, James. *Notes of a Native Son* (Boston: Beacon Press, 1984), 3.

5.   Allison, Dorothy. *Two or Three Things I Know for Sure* (New York: Penguin, 1996), 1.

6.   Twain, Mark. *Adventures of Huckleberry Finn* (Berkeley: University of California Press, 2001), 1–2.

7.   Martin, Lee. *The Bright Forever* (New York: Three Rivers Press, 2006), 4.

8.   Martin, Lee, in "The Long Light of Prose: An Interview with Lee Martin," *Newfound* (Vol. 6, Issue 1, 2015). https://newfound.org/archives/volume-6/issue-1/interviews-lee-martin

9.   Martin, Lee. "Close to Home: Writing the Small and the Intimate," Lee Martin blog, October 12, 2015. http://leemartinauthor.com/2015/10/close-to-home-writing-the-small-and-the-intimate/

10. Menand, Louis. "Bad Comma," *New Yorker*, June 28, 2004, 102.

11. Dickens, Charles. *Great Expectations* (Boston: Estes and Lauriat, 1881), 26.

12. Haddon, Mark. T*he Curious Incident of the Dog in the Night-Time* (New York: Vintage, 2004), 1.

13. Baum, L. Frank. *The Wonderful Wizard of Oz* (Chicago: George M. Hill Co., 1900), 12–13.

14. Doyle, Brian. *The Wet Engine: Exploring the Mad Wild Miracle of the Heart* (Brewster, MA: Paraclete Press, 2005), 1–2.

15. Martin, in "The Long Light of Prose."

16. Rowling, J. K., cited in Garrison Keillor's *The Writer's Almanac*, July 31, 2013. http://writersalmanac. publicradio.org/index.php?date=2013/07/31

6 | The Strong Skeleton

1. Hemingway, Ernest. *Death in the Afternoon* (New York: Scribner Reprint Edition, 1996), 116.

2. Dickens, *David Copperfield*, 9.

3. Strayed, Cheryl. *Wild: From Lost to Found on the Pacific Crest Trail* (New York: Alfred A. Knopf, 2012), 3.

4. Borich, Barrie Jean. *Body Geographic* (Lincoln: University of Nebraska Press, 2013), 20.

5. Adams, Douglas. *The Long, Dark Tea-Time of the Soul* (New York: Gallery Books, 1988), 119.

6. Lamott, quoted in Susan Wittig Albert, *An Extraordinary Year of Ordinary Days*, 173.

7. Bradbury, Ray. "Day at Night: Ray Bradbury," *Day at Night*, City University of New York Television, January 21, 1974. www.cuny.tv/show/dayatnight/PR1012346

8. Straub, Peter. "A Conversation with Benjamin Percy," *Amazon.com Reviews*. www.amazon.com/ Red-Moon-Benjamin-Percy/dp/145554535X

7 | Keeping Fit

1. Didion, Joan. "Why I Write," *New York Times*, December 5, 1976, 2, 98.

8 | An Apple a Day

1. Plath, Sylvia. *The Journals of Sylvia Plath* (New York: Anchor Books, 1998), 85.

2. Allende, "Why I Write," 6.

3. Bausch, Richard. "Letter to a Young Writer," National Endowment for the Arts. www.arts.gov/operation-homecoming/essays-writing/letter-young-writer

4. Tharp, Twyla. *The Creative Habit: Learn It and Use It for Life* (New York: Simon & Schuster, 2006), 162–163.

5. Edison, Thomas, cited in "How Failure Taught Edison to Repeatedly Innovate," *Forbes.com*, June 9, 2011. www.forbes.com/sites/nathanfurr/2011/06/09/how-failure-taught-edison-to-repeatedly-innovate/ #7ccdc0b738f5

6. Keyes, Ralph. *The Writer's Book of Hope: Getting from Frustration to Publication* (New York: Henry Holt, 2003), 85.

7. Ibid., 142.

8. Alcott, Louisa May. *The Selected Letters of Louisa May Alcott* (Athens, GA: University of Georgia Press, 1995), 308.

9. Saunders, George. *The Braindead Megaphone* (New York: Riverhead, 2007), 55.

9 | The Book Doctor's Final Illegible Scribbles

1. Kennedy, Mark. "Alan Rickman Returns to Broadway with Attitude," Associated Press, November 18, 2011.

2. Asimov, Janet, and Isaac Asimov. *How to Enjoy Writing: A Book of Aid and Comfort* (New York: Walker, 1987), 51.

Acknowledgments

This book would never have been possible without the lessons I've learned wrestling book ideas and stalled drafts alongside so many brilliant students, especially those I've met in repeat visits to the *Kenyon Review* Summer Writing Workshops, the San Miguel de Allende Writers' Conference, and the *Creative Nonfiction* Writers' Conference.

Thanks as well to my generous teachers, including Caroline Hammer, Lee Gutkind, Romulus Linney, David Bradley, James Gordon Bennett, Vance Bourjaily, Kate Daniels, Rodger Kamenetz, and Moira Crone. The colored highlighter exercise at the end of chapter 3 is a variation on a show-not-tell exercise often taught by Lee Gutkind, and I thank him for that.

My colleagues at Ohio University have been endlessly generous and continue to teach me new lessons. A special shout-out to Bob and Kate, Eric and Kristin, and Roland. My students at Ohio University are insanely talented as well, and wonderful.

Lisa Westmoreland at Ten Speed Press is a genius editor, and Carol Mann continues to be a supportive agent with keen wit and discernment.

Finally, heartfelt thanks to my daughter Maria, my wife Renita, and whoever it was that first thrust a pencil into my hand.

About the Author

PHOTO © RENITA ROMASCO

Dinty W. Moore is the director of the MA and PhD in Creative Writing programs at Ohio University. He is the author of *Dear Mister Essay Writer Guy: Advice and Confessions on Writing, Love, and Cannibals*, the memoir *Between Panic & Desire*—winner of the Grub Street Nonfiction Book Prize—and many other books. Moore has published fiction and nonfiction in the *Southern Review*, the *Georgia Review*, *Harpers*, the *New York Times Sunday Magazine*, *Arts & Letters*, and the *Normal School*, among other venues. He lives in Athens, Ohio.

Index

ALSO BY DINTY W. MOORE

Dear
MISTER ESSAY
WRITER GUY

This unconventional writing guide in the form
of a witty, tongue-in-cheek advice column features
contributions from Cheryl Strayed, Phillip Lopate,
Roxane Gay, and more!

With a tip of the hat to history's most infamous
essay—Montaigne's "Of Cannibals"—this book
provides rollicking relief for writers in distress.

Hardcover ISBN: 978-1-60774-809-0
E-book ISBN: 978-1-60774-810-6

Available from TEN SPEED PRESS
wherever books are sold.
www.tenspeed.com

Copyright © 2017 by Dinty W. Moore

Published in the United States by Ten Speed Press,
an imprint of the Crown Publishing Group, a division
of Penguin Random House LLC, New York.
www.crownpublishing.com
www.tenspeed.com

Ten Speed Press and the Ten Speed Press colophon are
registered trademarks of Penguin Random House LLC.

Library of Congress Cataloging-in-Publication Data
Names: Moore, Dinty W., 1955- author.
Title: The story cure : a book doctor's pain-free guide to finishing your
    novel or memoir / Dinty W. Moore.
Description: Berkeley : Ten Speed Press, 2017. | Includes bibliographical
    references and index.
Identifiers: LCCN 2016036789 (print) | LCCN 2016055182 (e-book) |
Subjects: LCSH: Fiction—Authorship. | Fiction—Technique. |
    Autobiography—Authorship. | Creative writing. | BISAC: LANGUAGE
ARTS & DISCIPLINES / Composition & Creative Writing. | LANGUAGE
ARTS & DISCIPLINES / Grammar & Punctuation. | LANGUAGE ARTS &
DISCIPLINES / Reference.
Classification: LCC PN3355 .M66 2017 (print) | LCC PN3355 (e-book) | DDC
    808.3—dc23
LC record available at https://lccn.loc.gov/2016036789

Trade Paperback ISBN: 978-0-399-57880-9
E-book ISBN: 978-0-399-57881-6

Printed in the United States of America

Front cover illustration of open book by CreativeMarket.com/ssstocker
Design by Tatiana Pavlova

10 9 8 7 6 5 4 3 2 1

First Edition